Susannah

Our Incredible 114-Year-Old Aunt

BY

DR. LAVILLA MUSHATT WATSON

the Peppertree Press

Sarasota, Florida

For information regarding permission,
call 941-922-2662 or contact us at our website:
www.peppertreepublishing.com or write to:
the Peppertree Press, LLC.
Attention: Publisher
1269 First Street, Suite 7
Sarasota, Florida 34236

ISBN: 978-1-61493-222-2

Library of Congress Number: 2013919668

Printed in the U.S.A.

Printed January 2014

Dedication

Tee, for your love,
encouragement, and generosity,
we thank you and we love you.

Your Family

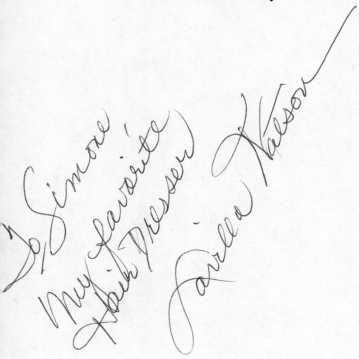

*To Simone!
My favorite
Hair Dresser*

Jarrell Watson

ACKNOWLEDGEMENTS

To my children, Audrey and Russell please know how grateful I am for your support and computer expertise. For give me for disrupting your lives when my level of frustration with modern day technology moved into the realm of insanity. Thank you for your constructive suggestions and great ideas. Bless you for the many times one of you rescued Zachary and Brooke's grandma.

I am truly thankful to my siblings and other members of the family who enthusiastically shared their memories of Aunt Tee. To my sister Lois, thank you for allowing me to hear your crisp pleasant voice anytime of day or night I needed your opinion or wanted to discuss some issue regarding Tee. Doris, you have known Tee as long as I have and you often shared stories about her that I had forgotten. Thank you so much for holding on to your long term memories and for sharing them with me. What would I do without my siblings?

Selbra, you always enjoy sharing with me our Aunt Tee's reaction when the three of you arrive on Sundays with her favorite home made dishes. I love to hear these intimate tidbits about her life, and I want you to know how much I appreciate it. I am so proud of you, Doris and Lois, whom I refer to as Tee's "Earthly Angels," for your personal sacrifices and devotion to our only surviving aunt. Thanks so much for doing what you can to keep Tee safe, healthy and happy.

Mac, you have shared some interesting stories about Tee that you learned over the many years you have known her. I want you to know how valuable that information was to me in developing the history of her life. Thank you and Valerie for your continued involvement in Tee's life.

I thank my dear friend Lucy Hedrick, the author of five self-help books, who took the time to read my book proposal, made suggestions, and referred me to the appropriate literary experts.

To Harvey Webb JR. D. D. S., M. M. H., author of WASH, a historical novel, I appreciate your sending me to Donna Lee Gould. Her recommendations were invaluable and just what I needed to move forward in finishing my book. Harvey, I am so happy that you sent me to check out the Peppertree Press when I was looking for a publisher. Julie Ann Howell greeted me as though we were old friends as she invited me into her cozy office. I knew immediately that I had met the person who would take a personal as well as a professional interest in my Aunt Susannah's life history. Thank you!

Special thanks to Donna Lee Gould for evaluating my manuscript. The time I spent with you was most helpful for you high lighted areas of incontinences as well as the need for better organization in other areas of my manuscript. I left you feeling more secure about how to make my book more appealing to the average reader.

INTRODUCTION

Susannah, affectionally called Tee, is written as a tribute to our aunt and hopefully an inspiration to others. It is an honor to have been touched by her love and generosity throughout our lives. We are proud and delighted as a family to share the life story of a woman who at age 114 is one of the world oldest people. The aim of this book is to leave a written record of her legacy for future generations, who will be inspired by her strength, audacious personality, and her love for her family.

Susannah portrays the early life of a young girl growing up on a farm in the south with her parents and ten siblings. Her parents struggled to send Tee to boarding school, and when she graduated, was the first in her family to receive a high school diploma. This bright, ambitious youngster loved working with young children and dreamed of becoming a teacher. She had to abandon her dream because her parents were poor sharecroppers who didn't have the money to send her to college. Determined to rescue her family from the strong grips of poverty, Tee took a domestic housekeeping job in the north. The book gives the reader a flavor of this young lady's courage and determination to travel miles away from home during the early 1900s to help support her family.

Susannah will take readers on a forty-five year journey in the work world of domestic housekeeping and childcare in the north. The book will reveal stories about families Tee worked for and the children she loved and nurtured. She had a remarkable work history and developed outstanding culinary skills. Although she never earned a lot of money on any of her jobs, she sent most of what she earned to her family, always remembering to send gifts and clothing to the children.

The book discusses Tee's involvement in church, clubs, and other humanitarian activities. There are discussions about her personal struggles and periods of loneliness, yet good times in her life as she worked to pave the path for others to have a better life. *Susannah* helps readers to look into the heart of a woman of great strength who maintained a perspective on what and how she wanted to spend her life. Though not politically active, she worked to raise funds for worthy causes. Having been denied the opportunity to pursue her education motivated Tee and her schoolmates from Alabama to raise money and scholarships for disadvantaged Black students in the 1950s. *Susannah* goes on to recount how passionate Tee was to see every young person get an education and improve their standard of living. Tee managed to help three nieces to go to college and encouraged other relatives to come north to work.

Susannah will not only discuss issues related to Tee's longevity, but her legacy, a treasure to leave for future generations. It will reveal and preserve the essence of Tee's life, her impeccable character, dependability and compassion for all people. *Susannah* will serve as a gift to family members and a joyful inspirational experience for others. Readers will discover that this intelligent, witty, sassy woman loves to laugh and enjoys social gatherings with family and friends.

The book will show that Tee surrounded herself with good friends, worked hard, took care of herself and had a long, healthy, happy retirement. The happiest years of her life, she says, came after she retired. Four decades later, Tee continued to enjoy good health, and still looks forward to family gatherings, and socializing with her decreasing group of friends.

Susannah recounts a series of comical, sometimes painful episodes that will give readers a glimpse of Tee's struggles with the aging process. This strong, independent, humorous woman with the hearty laughter maintained her autonomy as long she as could. For some individuals, it will be a soul-wrenching experience to watch this intrepid trooper relinquish some of her control.

Susannah will offer readers, particularly retiring Baby Boomers and their families, a peek into age-related social, medical, and psychological issues. As we observed with our Aunt Tee, at some point, it will become imperative for someone to coordinate and advocate on behalf of elderly relatives. While *Susannah* discusses a range of issues that Tee struggled with, need for control, independence, indecisiveness, and other personal perks are applicable to most elderly individuals. One thing they'll have in common though is their day-to-day physical, psychological, and emotional needs. More than anything, our aunt wanted the love and involvement of her family.

TABLE OF CONTENTS

Sitting on the steps of her sister's house
in Mt. Vernon, NY circa 1939

CHAPTER 1
GROWING UP IN ALABAMA

*Childhood experiences leave blueprints on our
hearts and souls for future references.*

Behind the brick and mortar walls in one of New York's Public Senior Housing Developments lives a 114-year-old legend, my aunt Susannah, affectionately called Tee. This documentation of her life is a tribute to her and an inspiration for others.

During the early 1920s Tee left her family and the fields of Alabama to go north to work as a domestic homemaker. She knew as a young girl that she wanted to be an educator but had to abandon her plans because her parents were poor sharecroppers who could not afford to send her to college. Tee dedicated her life to helping others achieve their dreams, assisting three nieces as well as many others to go to college. Now she spends her days in her small apartment softly rocking in her lounge chair. Sometimes she hums one of her favorite songs as she patiently waits for the two things that gives her great joy, mealtime and visits from her family. Some of the other great pleasures of her long life have been diminished as the cruel ravages of the aging process occur. Sometimes we hear Tee commenting to herself, "Oh boy, I am old and I am so tired." She is blind, hard of hearing, wheelchair bound, and requires around the clock care.

The only surviving grandchild of emancipated slaves, Stephen and Ann Mushatt, Tee was born July 6, 1899, in Lowndes County,

1

Alabama, the third oldest of eleven children, all deceased. Her parents, Callie and Mary Mushatt, were lifetime sharecroppers who stayed in the same community tilling the same soil as Tee's grandparents when they were slaves. Tee and her siblings grew up in a small community surrounded by a large, close-knit family of grandparents, uncles, aunts, and numerous cousins. Their neighbors were also sharecroppers with large families.

When the young people of Tee's generation became adults, some stayed in Alabama and became sharecroppers. They were unable to become landowning farmers because they could not secure loans to purchase farm animals and equipment needed for farming. Other men and women left home to seek employment in large cities and states, where they found jobs in construction and log rolling, as porters and cooks, and in housekeeping. The only available work for "Colored" people at that time was farming, clearing the land, and caring for livestock. Tee, a bright, ambitious youngster was determined she was not going to live and work on a farm the rest of her life. She said, "I never liked working in the fields and usually found some excuse why I couldn't go out in that hot sun. I stayed home to cook and care for the very young children." Farming was not her dream, and she made it her goal as a young girl to somehow break the cycle of sharecropping that had trapped her family in poverty.

During the 18th Century, up to the period shortly after the Emancipation Proclamation of 1865, when slaves were freed, there were large tracts of undeveloped swamp land for sale in Lowndes County, Alabama. Wealthy northerners flocked to this part of the south seeking a warmer climate for their slaves and farm land to expand their plantations. Lowndes County was noted for its dark fertile soil, conducive for growing a number of crops such as cotton, corn, potatoes, tobacco, peas, peanuts, and sugar cane. With plenty of money and slave labor, the slave owners built large mansions for themselves and their families and small log cabins for their slaves.

In 1840, Tee's grandfather, a young boy named Stephen, was among the nineteen slaves who were brought to Alabama from Statesville, North Carolina, by Dr. John Mushatt and his family. Steven met Ann McCray, a young woman from one of the local Cherokee Indian tribes in Alabama. According to the 1890 Census, the couple married in 1863. Ann lost her first two young children to croup and pneumonia. Based on archives' death records the high mortality rate of infants born in the 1890s was due to pneumonia and the croup. The adults usually died from pneumonia and tuberculosis. Lack of medical care and substandard and overcrowded living quarters were contributing factors.

Stephen and Ann subsequently had thirteen more children, all born after slavery was abolished. Ann was forty-three years old when her last child was born in 1893. Stephen lived to be eighty-nine. Ann died at the home of one of her daughters in Lowndes County, Alabama, at the age of 101.

Ironically, many of the freed salves were worse off after slavery was abolished, because now they had no work and no way of finding work. No one would hire them; many families were asked to vacate their cabins. Some of the former slave owners claimed that the freed slaves owed them money for the years they clothed and fed them and their families. The freed slaves were trapped, in debt, and on the brink of starvation. For years a great number of families lived under severe, impoverished conditions until their children were old enough to leave home, find jobs, and begin helping their families.

According to Tee and her siblings, Stephen and Ann were offered a place to stay on their former owner's plantation at no cost for the rest of the lives. Stephen declined the offer, and moved off the plantation, rented land from another landowner, and became a lifetime sharecropper, a status just above that of a slave.

When his grandchildren talk about Stephen and his relationship with his former master, we get a picture of a man who was a trusted slave who had a pretty good relationship with his master. Stephen, for example, was in charge of the other slaves on the plantation, he had been with the same master since he was a little boy, and had never tried to run away from the plantation. We suspect Stephen was the benefactor of special privileges in the form of money and/or land to live on if he chose to stay. Did Stephen not trust his former master? According to his grandchildren, Stephen not only wanted his freedom, he wanted his independence and he wanted to support his family. He cared deeply about the family. He tried to instill in his children and grand children the importance of having something of their own, such as land and a home that no one could take away from them.

Tee loved to talk about her grandparents, always with a big smile on her face: "Oh, my grandfather was a big, strong, tall, handsome man, way over six feet. He could carry a good-size tree on his shoulder." She would look around to see who else was listening and whisper, "Your daddy looks just like his father and grandfather." Stephen, it appears, worked very hard and took good care of his family. He was affectionate and enjoyed interacting with his grandchildren. Tee was very attached to her grandmother Ann, who was not as affectionate and patient with some of her grandchildren, who thought of her as sometimes mean. When Tee got into trouble with her mother, she ran to find her favorite grandmother for comfort and cuddling.

Interestingly, Stephen never discussed his parents or his early years growing up. We don't know if his mother traveled with him from North Carolina to Alabama with those nineteen slaves or if she was sold to another slave owner. At some point someone remembered that Stephen thought that his parents Horace and Mary were from Africa.

Tee's parents, Mary and Callie, married in 1892. They, like many of their friends and neighbors, built a small log cabin and lived in the same community close to their families. Over the years, the couple had eleven children, five boys and six girls. The living quarters consisted of one to two room log cabins constructed from clapboard siding, sometimes brick. More rooms were added as the family increased. A central fireplace for cooking and heating was the family's gathering place after the day's end or when the weather outside forced all to huddle against the elements. Wooden shudders would shut out the wind and the light and wrap the fire's warmth around them. Fireplaces were built with a couple of long hooks extending from the opened chimney for hanging pots over the fire. Iron pots were essential for cooking foods that required many hours to cook such as meats, stews, and especially wild animals.

Tee's family was Baptist, so she became a member until she went north. Grandma Mary, her mother, and the young children attended church on a regular basis. Grandpa Callie and the boys, once they became teenagers, found other things to do on Sunday. Every Sunday Grandma loaded her girls in their one-horse buggy and drove those four mile to Mt. Olive A. M. E. Zion Baptist Church located in a community at that time called Tyson.

During cold winter days when it was too cold for the children to play outside, or go to school, Tee and her siblings sat around the fire and played dominoes and homemade games, cooked peanuts, popcorn, and sweet potatoes and ate pecans and walnuts they had collected from the woods in the neighborhood. Occasionally, the siblings had disagreements and fights. When the teasing and disagreements got out of control, Grandma Mary intervened. She was the disciplinarian who could bring the situation under control with just the threat of a whipping if the fighting and arguing didn't stop. Grandpa Callie assumed a gentler, protective role with his children. He never whipped them because he could not bear to see them in pain. Tee said that her father would not allow their Grandmother Cindy to whip his children because she whipped them too long and she made the boys pull down their pants so she could hit them on their bare butts. Not only was this act painful, it was utterly humiliating for his boys. This experience may have brought back memories of how slaves were treated.

Grandpa Callie died in 1931 at age sixty two. He was a proud grandfather of one grandson Frank, whom he and the family adored. Sadly, he died within months of the second grandson's and the first granddaughter's births. Three teenagers and a ten-year-old still lived at home at the time of his death. The second oldest daughter, Lavilla, was married and lived in another community. Sadly, at only twenty-four, she died of tuberculosis after two brief years of marriage.

Grandma Mary was now fifty-six, in poor health, and unable to work on the farm. She became totally dependent on help from her young adult children, some of whom had families of their own to support. For example, my parents, Callie and Bettie, were expecting their first child, as was Aunt Verbena and her husband, Monroe. The Great Depression had just begun and Tee, now living in New York, was the only member in the family who had a job and regularly sent every dollar she could spare back home to support the family.

Tee's mother had no idea that her daughter earned so little amount of money. Her demands for more money continued despite the fact that Tee was sending money to her married siblings when she could. Tee shared that "the needs and health conditions of my family were always on my mind." She continued, "The minute I received my pay, always in cash, I would walk rather than take a cab to the post office to mail my mother a money order." Whatever amount of money she sent her mother was never enough. Someone always needed something. She would ask the ones still at home to "write to Susannah and ask her to send me more money."

As Tee talked about her mother's demands I got the impression from the tone of her voice that Grandma Mary never gave Tee the praise or recognition for being such a wonderful, generous daughter who literally kept her family from starving during the Depression. Tee, I believe, felt hurt and angry over her mother's lack of gratitude and rarely spoke of those troubling years. The pain of not being appreciated by her mother did hurt her. However, down through the years she seems to have toned down her anger and perhaps forgave her mother. When Tee starts to talk about that period, she looks away, and comments, "That period was the saddest time in my life. I lived each day expecting sad news from home that something bad had happened to someone in my family. You see, I had lost two sisters, Lavilla and Lecettie, my father, and my brother Hardie was missing; all of this happened within a few years." Tee said that it made her feel very proud to help her family. "Thank God for keeping me strong and healthy during those difficult times." She'll look at me with pride in her voice—"did you know that I have never been sick?" When Tee opened up about her feelings during her working years, she was in her seventies and living with me and my family. She was apparently happy, and had time to reflect on the journey she had traveled.

After the death of Grandpa Callie, my father Callie Jr., and his two brothers, Cody and George, assumed responsibility for the farm and helped their mother raise their younger siblings. My father worked odd jobs to earn enough money to buy farm items and equipment, and each year reaped an ample harvest for

7

his mother and his own family. My mother had a child every two years, while continuing to help my father on the farm. Those early years of successful farming, while struggling to support two families, gave my parents the confidence that they could earn a living at farming.

Life on the farm in rural Alabama during the early nineteen hundreds was pretty boring. For young people, especially teenagers, there was little time for socializing, very little if any reading material, no radio, television, or telephones. One day seemed to roll into another, chores and activities changed with the seasons. Because of duties on the farm, many youngsters could not plan on starting school on time. School and church were the only places where young people had a little time to interact with each other. The most difficult work arose from April through October, when families worked out in the fields. Girls who could get to school were allowed to do so from October to April. Boys were needed a month longer to finish harvesting the crops. They had to leave school early in March to prepare the fields for spring planting.

School attendance was sporadic and the drop-out rate extremely high. Many students didn't start school until they were eight or nine years old. There were men and women during that time who never went to school. They were illiterate all of their lives. The boys were the first to drop out because after a couple of years they were academically so far behind their female peers. Unfortunately, ninety percent of Negroes during this period in history could not read or write and therefore were unable to assist their children. Parental illiteracy contributed to some of the numerous errors and discrepancies in dates of births and other pertinent family data. Some of the parents had just come through a period in their lives when it was a crime to teach "Coloreds" to read, whether they were slaves or free. Frequently, parents were beaten by their landlord or run off their property for sending their children to school. However, there was always someone in the community who was blessed with a good memory and some basic reading skills.

Tee and her siblings were born at home, delivered by women in the community who had never gone to school, but had acquired birthing skills. Today these women are known as midwives. Many are trained licensed practitioners who work in hospitals and birthing centers. In the rural area where Tee was born the birth of a child was frequently not recorded with the Department of Vital Statistics until the census recorders placed the child in the record some eight or nine years later. Birthdays for the most part were recorded based on what the parents could remember. In some cases, births were never recorded. For example, Georgia, one of Tee's, sisters, sustained a fatal blow from a horse when she was nine. Since Georgia was born after the 1900 Census, but before the 1910 Census, her birth was never recorded. When Tee applied for Social Security Benefits at age sixty-five, no record of her birth could be found. Since her birth was never recorded with the Alabama Office of Vital Statistics, she was never issued a birth certificate. To qualify for Social Security she had to secure notarized statements from three individuals who knew when she was born. Several decades later while researching the family, eleven-month-old "Susannah" and her family were found in the 1900 Census.

CHAPTER 2

TEE GOES AWAY TO BOARDING SCHOOL

*This is my opportunity to get an education
and leave Alabama.*

Tee and her siblings attended elementary school in a one-room, windowless, dilapidated building that also served as a church on Sunday. The teachers were not college educated, but young women who had finished high school and taken some college courses. The students were taught classes in reading, writing, spelling, and arithmetic. The school was within walking distance from their home and was open only three months of the year to allow the young people to work in the fields during farming season. In the surrounding communities, there were several of these poorly constructed buildings that were places of worship on Sunday that converted to schools during the week. Parents and churches supplied labor and building materials, while the Freedmen's Bureaus and The American Missionary Society provided funds, buildings, and salaries for the teachers. The Freedmen's Bureau was a government agency set up to assist freed slaves with their transition from slavery to freedom.

These community schools taught first through sixth grade. Due to the high dropout rate, very few students completed sixth grade. Tee was among the few students who were promoted to the seventh grade in 1917.

Tee's dream of going to college to become a teacher was known by her parents and her teachers. She was clearly qualified, for she was a very bright, ambitious young woman with an excellent academic record. From her teacher, she learned about the possibility of going for her high school diploma, which she needed to go on to college. Her comments about that period were characteristic of what Tee would say: "I knew that my parents didn't have the money to even send me to high school, never mind college. But I had faith and I prayed for God to help me find a way to fulfill my dreams, so that I could help my family and educate children."

One of the teachers at Tee's school gave her an application to apply for admission to The Calhoun Colored School, the only high school for "Coloreds" in the area at that time. The school was founded by Dr. Booker T. Washington in 1892. Dr. Washington was a graduate of Hampton Normal and Agricultural Institute, and founder of Tuskegee Institute. In addition to the support and guidance from other Black scholars such as Dr. W. E. B. Du Bois and Jesse Jones, the school was funded by parents, private groups, and several philanthropic organizations. The school was established specially to educate "Colored" children because there were no public funds allocated by the county or state for their education. Tee's parents and their contemporaries, though illiterate, knew the value of an education and desperately wanted their children to enjoy the world of literacy.

When Tee told her parents that she had applied for admission to go to the Calhoun Colored School, they told her how proud they were of her, and promised to help her in any way they could. Fortunately, the first four or five years prior to Tee applying to boarding school farmers in the area had reaped bountiful crops, especially cotton, which allowed farmers to clear up all of their debts with a few dollars to spare. Tee's parents felt that they were in a position to pay Tee's board and tuition. Also, students were expected to work on campus as part of their training experience. The school encouraged parents who didn't have enough cash to cover their children's board and tuition, to use the barter system. On several occasions during Tee's tenure at school, her parents couldn't pay for her school's expenses because they didn't have enough money. Their crops were destroyed by a severe drought one year and a couple of years later by a rainy summer. Tee's father would take his sons into the woods and haul wagon loads of wood to the school to cover the cost of the tuition. At other times parents brought fresh produce or gave a few days of human labor, using whatever skills they had; working on the school's farm, gardening, and working in the carpentry shop. Parents who had some schooling also volunteered several days tutoring young children in the classroom.

The Calhoun Colored School, later called The Calhoun School, offered a vigorous academic program for students beginning in kindergarten up through adulthood. A school year consisted of ten months. Students received a high school diploma after completing the tenth grade. With this diploma and good grades they were accepted at several prestigious colleges and universities. The Calhoun School offered courses in algebra, writing, sewing, laundering, and cooking for girls. The program for boys included courses in agriculture, carpentry, blacksmithing, and shoe making. Later, other courses such etiquette; beauty culture, and personal grooming were added. The school environment offered an array of life experiences and skills that students could not have acquired anywhere in the south at that time in history. For example, students developed work ethics, good study habits, discipline, personal grooming, and community values.

Tee adjusted well at school. As a matter of fact, she said that she was energized by the rigorous academic program and meeting people who shared her passion for knowledge. She said, "I was living part of my dream, rising every morning at the sound of the 5 a.m. bell to finish my chores before class." Her daily schedule, which ended at 9 each night, was a challenge but she was determined to earn her high school diploma. Earning a high school diploma in the early 20th Century was a great achievement for a "Colored" student.

At the time, students received a high school diploma after they completed tenth grade. Tee was the first in her family to finish high school.

At boarding school, Tee enjoyed interacting with her classmates from other towns and communities. Some of the young men and women she met at school became lifetime friends. The school year was from September to April. During the summer she went home to work on the farm and help care for her younger siblings. She always had mixed feelings when it was time to return to school because there was so much work left to do on the farm. Returning to school late was not an option because of her chores and academic schedule.

One day while Tee was away at boarding school, her brother Callie showed up and told her that their brother Hardie had gotten into some trouble and had to leave home. He had allegedly killed a man in self-defense. Tee remembered crying herself to sleep many nights wondering what would happen to her brother. She knew that her parents were not going to allow Hardie to go to jail because there was a possibility that they would never see him again. This part of the country had a history of brutalizing and sometimes murdering colored males for committing minor offences.

The family learned that Hardie was alive some thirty years ago when one of our cousins met a man at a family gathering in Mississippi. The gentleman resembled his father, George, and my father, Callie. Our cousin whose name is also Hardie (named for his uncle Hardie), approached the gentleman giving his full name and place of resident as Alabama. The gentleman's face lit up with a big smile but quickly walked away and disappeared in the crowd. Several years later, we pursued the matter and verified that the gentleman was indeed my father's brother Hardie. He was difficult to locate because he had changed his name and the date of his birth. Uncle Hardie was known as Sampson Oner, married and the father of three children. He died in 1973 at the age of eighty-three.

According to his children, Hardie had lived and worked in the southern part of the country, either in Mississippi or Louisiana, all of his life. For many years, he worked on the railroad, but after retirement, he farmed the several acres of land he had purchased over the years. A few years after meeting our cousins, we were invited to a family reunion in Mississippi to meet uncle Hardie's large family. We corresponded with the family on a regular basis for several years. In later years, we keep in touch once a year, usually during the holiday season.

Shortly after Hardie left Alabama, Tee's oldest brother, Elbert, whom we called Uncle Sonny left home looking for work and ended up in Birmingham, Alabama. He eventually married and started his family but stayed in touch with his family down in the country. After Elbert retired, he came to the country to see his family more frequently. He enjoyed sitting on the porch with his brothers Callie and George sharing childhood experiences. Elbert died at the age of eighty-seven in Birmingham.

My aunt was a friendly, well-mannered young woman who never got into any difficulty during her four-year tenure at school. Firstly, she was so proud and happy for this opportunity, and secondly, she couldn't disappoint her family, considering the painful sacrifices they were making for her.

On the eve of Saturday, March 4, 1922, at 7 p.m., Tee and twenty-one of her classmates, six males, and sixteen females, prepared to walk across the stage to receive a much-deserved, hard-earned high school diploma. The graduation ceremony took place under a grove of trees on the school's beautiful, well-manicured campus. Parents with heavy hearts, happy faces, and their best outfits were surrounded by an equally proud staff on this special occasion. The "Class Night" program consisted of speeches, songs, readings, and music. Each student played a role entertaining parents, staff, and distinguished guests. Tee's role was to give a reading on "Negro Music in France."

When Tee received her diploma that night, history was made. She was the first person in her family to receive a diploma. It was an accomplishment that made her family extremely happy. Having successfully achieved this long sought after dream was a liberating experience that lifted her spirit and gave her hope for a brighter future.

Shortly after graduation, Tee received two pieces of encouraging mail. One of the letters was from Tuskegee University Admissions Office advising her that she had been accepted in the Teacher's Education Program. This news was bittersweet because Tee knew that her parents could not afford to send her to college. It had been a tremendous financial burden on the family to get her through boarding school. Nonetheless, she was proud to have been accepted. Although Tee was very disappointed that the lack of money robbed her, and others, of something they badly wanted. The thought that "No child should be denied an education for lack of money" stayed with her. Tee vowed at that time to use her time and energy, and whatever money she could spare, to help those who wanted to get an education, starting with members of her family.

The second letter was from was from one of the local church

schools, offering her a position as a teacher assistant, which she gladly accepted. So, when school opened that fall after graduating Tee began working as a teacher's assistant, living at home and earning eight dollars a week. Two months into the school year, Aunt Tee realized that this was not the life she had envisioned. She wanted to be an educator but thought that it was best for her to get out of Alabama. She actually hated farm life and the lack of social and intellectual stimulation in the community for young people. Her experience at boarding school had provided her the courage and incentive to keep her dream of expanding her horizons and moving away from the farming community.

While Tee struggled with her lack of options, she received a letter from one of her classmates, a friend, Maude Brown. After graduation, Maude made her way to New Jersey and found a job working as a mother's helper. Maude had seen an advertisement placed by an agency that was looking for young girls interested in doing housework and child care. The agency would send the girl a train ticket to New Jersey and place her with a family. The cost of the train ticket would be deducted from the girl's weekly salary until the bill was paid. Maude didn't tell Tee what the weekly salary was; she just wanted to know whether Tee was interested in this kind of work.

Tee tossed and turned for several nights, unable to sleep trying to decide firstly if she wanted to do the kind of work this job required, and secondly how was she going to approach her parents about leaving home. The only time she lived away from home was to attend boarding school, which was a distance of eight miles. Now twenty-two, the ambitious, intelligent young woman was prepared to convince her parents that this was the opportunity she needed to help the family, especially her younger siblings. My Aunt Tee decided that she was not going to ask her parents for permission to leave; she only wanted their blessing, which they readily gave. Her father seemed more concerned about Tee living so far away from her family. His words to her were, "Remember, you can always come back home if the job don't work out." Grandma Mary didn't have anything to say but had that concerned look on her face. Perhaps she had some reservations about her oldest daughter leaving home but she didn't verbalize them. Grandma knew that her Susannah was a strong-willed, stubborn young lady who "had a mind of her own," and was not easily persuaded by the opinions of others.

The letter to Maude was in the mail the next day, thanking her for the information about the job and indeed she would accept the position. Although Tee still didn't know what her salary would be, she told Maude that she would be ready to go when the ticket arrived. Tee began to plan in her head what garments might be appropriate for her to wear up north. She knew that she didn't need many clothes because she would wear a uniform while working, which was a blessing because she only had a couple of warm outfits that were appropriate for the cold weather up north. It was the middle of November and already getting cool in Alabama. By the time she receive her ticket and travel to New Jersey it will be December and very cold.

The year was 1922, a period in history when it took up to three weeks for residents living in rural areas to get their mail. At the time, mail moved from cities and towns by rails and on dirt roads by buggy and or horseback. Because there was very little mail back then, the postman didn't come every day. When residents placed an outgoing letter in the mailbox, it could stay there for three or four days before the postman picked it up. On a typical RFD (rural free delivery) route, it was not unusual to find up to fifteen mailboxes lined up alongside the road in various stages of decline. Some residents walked up to five miles to get their mail. Neighbors frequently picked up each others' mail, especially during rainy seasons when roads and bridges were often washed away.

About two weeks after she mailed her response back to Maude, Tee or someone in the family met the postman every other day looking for that precious letter from New Jersey with the ticket. Finally, sometime during the third week the ticket arrived with instructions that someone would meet Tee at the train station and drive her to the employer's home. When Tee checked the train's scheduled dates of departure and arrival, she was surprised that it would take three days and two nights to travel from Alabama to New Jersey. She would need to pack a large nonperishable lunch and a few changes of clothes. She had only seen pictures of cities in the north in books and a few magazines which belonged to her teacher. The idea of living in a big city was both frightening and exciting. My aunt wouldn't know any of the people and had no idea how she would find her way around. Her friend Maude lived in the same city she was going to but though she had her address, she had no idea how to get there. Tee decided when the time came she would ask her employer for help. Her confidence returned when she thought about the nights she lay in her bed, unable to sleep, imagining working in one of those beautiful northern cities. Her fantasy was becoming a reality.

CHAPTER 3
TEE TRAVELS NORTH TO WORK

Riding on the rails of hope, fear, and uncertainty.

One early morning in December, 1922, Tee's thirteen-year-old brother, Callie drove her to the train in the family's buggy to catch the north-bound train. There was little conversation between them on that nine-mile ride to the station. She knew Callie was sad she was leaving, but he respected her decision. Although they were ten years apart, they had a close relationship. When Callie was a baby, Tee stayed home to care for him and the younger children while everyone else went to the fields. He was a sensitive, caring, young man who assumed responsibility for his young siblings. His older brothers Elbert and Hardie were already gone.

From the time he was a young boy, Callie assumed adult roles and responsibilities, looking after his mother, grandmother, his siblings, and in later years, some of his sibling's children. My father told us his dying mother made him promise to take care of his youngest brother, George, twenty-five years old at the time and living with his mother. She was worried about Uncle George, who had lost one of his legs hoboing. Grandma was concerned that he would have difficulty finding a job and supporting himself. But once George received his prosthesis, he had no difficulty working and supporting his family. The two brothers had a close father-son relationship and usually lived near each other. My father's nieces and nephews have fond memories of their

Uncle Callie, whom they called Uncle Boox.

As Tee and Callie waited for the train, he turned to look at her and told her to "take care of yourself and don't allow anybody to take advantage of you." He seemed to be worried that once she left, he could not protect her. Tee has talked about that day and his words to her many times over the years. It touched her deeply that he cared so much about her.

When she saw the sadness in her brother's face, she was filled with guilt. She was so caught up in her excitement of leaving, it never occurred to her how much the pain of her leaving would cause her family. Callie could hardly raise his hand to wave good-bye to her as she boarded the train. She could no longer hold back the tears as she thought about how much she would miss her family that had loved and nurtured her for the last twenty-two years. She was leaving behind her parents, siblings, grandparents, aunts, uncles, cousins, friends, and neighbors. Despite her internal agony, my aunt was convinced she was doing the right thing. There was no turning back now; she was on he way. This was Tee's first train ride.

She finally settled down and began to enjoy the ride and the scenery as the train picked up speed. Although it was now December, some of the trees in Alabama still held onto some of their leaves. Tee had no idea how smooth the train ride was compared to the rough, shaky ride in a wagon. It finally occurred to Tee that there were several passengers already on the train. The train had originated in New Orleans and picked up a number of passengers along the way. Or course the passengers in her car, which was the first car, were Coloreds, some traveling with small children. During the 1920s, "Coloreds" were not allowed to ride in the same Pullman cars or eat in the dinning cars with white passengers. People of color traveling long distances knew to pack enough food to last until they reached their destination. An ideal lunch consisted of homemade biscuits, cake, fried chicken, saltine crackers, and maybe some fruit. The Pullman Porter provided a pitcher of water and paper cups for passengers once or twice during the day. Passengers in the first car were the last to be served.

During the 19th Century, coal was used as fuel to run the big train engines. These engines generated hazardous smoke and other carcinogenic materials which came through the open windows of the train. Except for the noise coming from the engine and the frequent whistle blowing, the first car wasn't that uncomfortable during the winter months when the windows were closed.

Tee never forgot her first train ride headed north. The following statement describes that experience: "It was a nightmare of a lifetime. The train was noisy and rocky. I got very little sleep because each time the train came through a little town, or a railroad crossing, the conductor blew the whistle. The first couple of times I heard that whistle, I jumped up, frightened and confused. My heart was beating a mile a minute. I didn't know where I was or what was happening around me. Some of my fellow passengers never woke up, while others came out of their slumber, looked around with red eyes, confusion on their faces, and went back to sleep. Due to lack of sleep the night before, I napped off and on all the next day. The Pullman Porter saw me when I jumped up at one of those stops. I guess I must have looked confused. He came over to reassure me that he would let me know when the train arrived in Newark, New Jersey. That reassurance made me feel better."

When the train arrived in Washington, D.C., all passengers disembarked to board other trains. Passengers were allowed to sit anywhere now that they had passed the "Mason Dixon Line." This border historically marked the division between the northern and southern states during the 1800s and the American Civil

War era. Those with money regardless of color could now have their meals in the dining car. Tee said that her parents had given her their last few dollars and "I would not spend it on some food that I may not even like." She still had some food left and a seat all to herself. She chose not to go to the dining car.

A few minutes before the train arrived in Newark, the Pullman Porter came up to Tee to tell her that she would be getting off at the next stop. She felt a rush of excitement, not only because she was finally almost there, she realized that she felt some kind of closeness to the Porter. He had kept an eye on her and relieved some of her anxiety. She remembered feeling comfortable in the care of a clean-cut colored man in his navy uniform, with matching hat and white shirt. He tipped his hat and said good bye to her.

CALHOUN SCHOOL SONG
— Tune, "Come Thy Fount"

Where earth smiles and heaven rejoices
Here where nature sings in tunes
Let us raise our joyful voices
Let us sing thy praise Calhoun.

Pleasant are the morning hours
Happy is thy sunny noon
Joyful is thy evening hours
Bright thy stars serene thy moon

Happy we who here are drinking
Daily draughts from wisdom's well
Oh! Within whose hearts are thinking
Daily thoughts too deep to tell

Here we learn with skill to labor
Knowing work is life's best boon
Learn to help and serve our neighbor
Love and priceless blessing thine Calhoun

Ties that bind us soon must sever
Parting time comes all too soon
But we'll sing thy praises forever
Sing Calhoun, God bless Calhoun

The Early Years

The Calhoon School

Calhoun School Graduating Class of 1922

Class in Scoring - 1900s

Calhoun School Class in Carpentry early 1900s

Class in Cooking - 1900s

Best Wishes To Olla Clay!

Olla B. Clay in Calhoun Band

Mr. & Mrs. Richard Clay
Harold & Dorie Clay
Richard Clay, Jr.
Carl Clay
Aimanie Clay

Class Night - 1922
Saturday, March 4, 7:15 P.M.

Song: "Enlisted Soldier"

President's Address   Charles L. Williams
Unveiling of motto
Response for Ninth Grade   David Marsh
Class History   Albert Davis
Members of the Class and the Wil   Callie Golson
Prophecy   Arthur B. Johnson

Class Song

The Negro in the World War
The Negro in our Earlier Wars   Eva L. Garrison
The World War and a chance to fight   Flora Lewis
Colored Officers and Life at Camp   Novella Henderson
French and English Negro soldiers   Nellie Mckee

Song: Trio, "The Old Road"

Eva l. Garrison, Maggie Mushatt, Gelene Gregory

The 92nd Division   Juanita Griggs
The 92nd after the Armistice   Hawthorne Taylor
The Buffaloes   Seona Robinson
Reading: From Ralph W. Tyler   Gelene Gregory
The Old Fifteenth   Elliot McCray

Song: "Tenting on the old Camp Ground"

Our Troops and the French   China Robinson
Negro Music in France   Susie Mushatt
Stevedore and Pioneer   Mary Payne
The S.A.T.C. and R.O.T.C.   Susie Williams

Song: "Artillery Song"

German Propaganda   Lillie Butler
Liberty Loans and the Red Cross   Mary Hare
Negro Labor and Social Welfare Agencies   Maude Brown
Some Letters   Maggie Mushatt
The End   Bertha Bozeman
Song: "The Ship in the Sea"

Calhoun School Alumni Association first Reunion 1957
Detroit, Michigan

Calhoun School Alumni Association Reunion 1960 in Chicago

CHAPTER 4

TEE'S EMPLOYMENT HISTORY

Cooking, cleaning, and nurturing.

As Tee stepped off the train in Newark, New Jersey, for her first domestic housekeeping job, a gentleman addressed her as Susannah and introduced himself as her driver who would take her to the employer's home. Everything went well. She was given three uniforms and told that her salary was seven dollars a week minus two dollars a week for her train ticket. Tee couldn't remember the cost of the train fare. For the first few weeks, she was very busy getting acquainted with a heavy work schedule. The family consisted of a young couple with two pre-school children. The father worked while mom stayed home. As it turned out, mom was seldom at home. She had an active social life, meeting with friends, attending luncheons and charitable events. In addition to caring for the children, Tee's other duties included cooking and serving the meals, doing the laundry, and cleaning the biggest house she had ever seen. Her employer taught her how and what grocery items to order for the family on a weekly basis. By the end of the day for the first three weeks, she was so exhausted she could barely make it up stairs to her sleeping quarters over the family's garage. Tee felt that once she became accustomed to the family's daily routine, the responsibilities would be easier to handle.

Tee's days off were every Thursday and every other Sunday. She didn't know anyone and had no place to go, so she stayed in her room to get some much needed rest. Letters to her family and Maude were in the mail to let them know that she had arrived safely. She had asked Maude to write back so that they could meet for lunch and catch up on how things were going in their individual lives.

It was now late February, 1923, and very cold in the north. Tee realized that she desperately needed warmer clothing when she went out. Maude took her shopping in one of the little shopping centers near Maude's job. Tee purchased a few items of clothing and her first winter coat from the money she had been saving. She had already sent her mother a couple of money orders. "I was filled with pride and joy to finally do something for my family," she said, fighting back tears because she didn't want me to see her crying.

Within a year of her arrival in New Jersey, Tee had fully paid her employer for the travel expenses. She had met a couple of ladies, also housekeepers, and began exploring the city of Newark as well as New York City. She heard that a middle-aged couple with no children was looking for a housekeeper. On one of her Thursdays off, she took the train into New York City for the interview.

The couple was impressed with Tee's experience, poise, and maturity. She was hired. This position turned out to be the ideal job for Tee as she only had to care for two people, and sometime later, a cat, Ginger. Tee's new employers, the Cokells, paid Tee a few dollars more than she was earning. Now she was earning ten dollars a week. Immediately, she knew that she was going to send more money to her family. The Cokells were a middle-aged, childless couple. Mr. Cokell was an executive with Paramount Pictures, traveled extensively, and was seldom at home. The couple gave elaborate parties for their friends and Mr. Cokell's business associates. They usually hired extra help to assist Tee with large social affairs in their home.

While working for the Cokells, Tee met and served a number of movie stars: Cary Grant, Ronald Reagan, George Raft, and Clarke Gable. She spent winters with the couple in Florida and California, where they had homes. She loved cooking for the Cokells because she had more time to plan some of her special dishes. Tee also enjoyed living in New York, where several friends and classmates now lived. After Mr. Cokell's death, his wife moved into a residence hotel in New York City. My aunt stayed with Mrs. Cokell for a few months to get her settled, and eventually accepted another sleep-in job in Westchester County. She had been with the Cokells sixteen years, and felt sad leaving this kind, elderly lady alone.

During her tenure as a domestic employee, especially with the Cokells, my aunt acquired extensive skills and knowledge of table setting and planning affairs for large formal dinners, as well as small supper parties. She honed her culinary skills from experimenting in the kitchen and reading cookbooks, beginning with Fannie Farmer, her first and most favorite cookbook. She added dozens of books to her collection over the years, but eventually gave many away as gifts. In later years, Tee sometimes planned the weekly menus for her employers, oftentimes creating her own recipes and specialty dishes. Planning large, elaborate parties gave my aunt an opportunity to display her creative genius with food. She truly enjoyed this aspect of her job and was so pleased with the positive feedback from her employers and their guests. We feel that cooking was one of Tee's special gifts that she enjoyed many years post-retirement. While working on these jobs she developed a love for beautiful china and silverware, exquisite glassware, and elegant table cloths.

For the majority of her working years, Tee lived in the homes of her employers. There were a few years during those years, though, when she rented an apartment in Mt. Vernon, a city close by, and took a cab home at night. At that time, she was married and living with her husband, Mr. Henry Jones, a gentleman whom she married in 1928. The marriage didn't last very long and the couple went their separate ways. Following their separation, Tee resumed her sleep-in pattern.

Tee had an outstanding work history. She got along well with most of her employers, who loved the way she treated their children. They were impressed with her work ethic, her honesty, her pride and, most certainly, her culinary skills. My aunt became attached to all the children she cared for, even if she didn't like their parents. The O'Donnell family was one of her favorite families. There were several young children and pets living in this big house. It required two full-time employees, a child-care worker, and a housekeeper to manage the lives of this active family. Tee stayed with this family long enough to see some of the children finish college and marry.

As soon as Tee terminated her employment with the O'Donnell family, she went up the street and worked for their neighbors, the Andrews. This couple had five children, a male infant and four girls which included a set of twins. Mrs. Andrews was a stay-at-home mom; Mr. Andrews worked in the city for a book publishing company. The Andrews also employed two full-time ladies, Tee and Miss Lulabelle, to help manage their home and care for their young children. Tee assumed a greater role caring for the children, while Lulabelle handled the cooking and other house duties. The two ladies were friends and I believe Miss. Lulabelle recruited my aunt to join her at the Andrews' house. Domestic housekeepers were noted for having an active and effective networking system. They relied on this method of communication to keep each other informed about where the jobs were, to gossip about their employers, and warn each other which employers to avoid.

My aunt worked for a half dozen or more employers during her work history, The Andrews family, I believe, was Tee's favorite family. Some fifty years after she terminated her employment with the family, the children are still in touch with her. They religiously call her and send her gifts and flowers on special occasions; her birthday, Mother's Day, and Christmas. Although the Andrews children are currently living in different states, they arranged to meet as a group at Tee's home on two occasions. Despite her age and poor memory, Tee can still recall all of the children's names in order of their birth: Gail, Carole, Joan, Jane, and Paul. She refers to them as "my children." When she gets angry with her nieces, she lashes out, "I am going to call the Andrews children and ask them to come and get me and take me to live with them." Everyone realizes that this outburst is one of Tee's methods of expressing her growing frustration and lack of control over her situation. She knows that the Andrews family genuinely loves her and will do almost anything for her. Paul calls her "his mother."

When Tee went to work for the Andrews, Paul was the first infant she had ever cared for on a job. He was this adorable, helpless creature that she instantly bonded with. Although she gave excellent care to the other children in the family, "Paul was her baby." There was something else different if not fascinating to Tee about this family. It was the novelty of caring for Joan and Jane, the Andrews' fraternal twins. While they may have many characteristics in common, they are individually unique. I think my aunt found it both challenging and exciting playing such an important role in the lives of these young girls.

According to my aunt, Mr. Andrews was perhaps the most thoughtful and likeable male employer during her tenure in this profession. She spoke of him as a kind, warm gentleman who always had something positive to say about the delicious meals she prepared for his family. He never forgot to thank her for staying in the kitchen to serve him on those nights when he arrived home late from work and missed having dinner with his family. Tee said "I will always remember with gratitude that had it not been for Mr. Andrews, I would not be getting Social Security today." Mr. Andrews was the first employer to arrange and pay Tee's payroll contributions to the Social Security System. At the time, during the fifties, no one was lobbying for the rights of domestic housekeepers. They were for many years, the silent, forgotten souls.

Sometime during the late fifties, Tee left the Andrews and worked for the Lembecks. By that time, the youngest child, Paul, was in school full time. My aunt never discussed why the Andrews let her go. Many years later when we asked her about it her response was "I don't want to talk about the reason I was let go because it made me so sad when I had to leave my children." We assumed that the Andrews didn't see the need for a full-time child care worker because their children were now in school all day.

The Lembecks were also neighbors of Tee's former employers. They were the parents of two preteen boys, Jamie and Peter. The boys didn't make any demands on Tee for attention as their mother was usually at home. However, the boys bonded with Tee and liked to hang out in the kitchen to chat with her about girls and dating. The Lembecks led a quite life, preferring to spend time at home with their boys and socializing with a small circle of friends. The Lembecks were not as wealthy as some of Tee's other employers.

After working for the Lembecks for 12 years, they let her go. The couple felt that they could no longer pay her salary and finance their boys education. This was a painful decision for everyone, especially the boys because they were so attached to Tee. My aunt was about 65- years old at the time, and rather than look for another job, decided to retire. Tee speaks fondly of the Lembecks, for she felt comfortable and relaxed in their home. Some years later, Mrs. Lembeck and one of her sons attended one of Tee's birthday parties, where she had a chance to meet Tee's large extended family.

When Tee talks about her years as a domestic employee, the stories are usually about the children. My aunt never had children of her own, but beginning with her childhood babysitting experiences, she honed just the right portion of love, discipline, warmth, and patience all children need and sometimes crave. She is an excellent disciplinarian who commands respect with the tone of her voice. When Tee gets angry, her voice tends to have the same effect on adults as it does on children; they back down and shut up!

On the job, Tee carried herself in a manner that made it easy for her employers to respect her. She never joked or shared personal information with her employers. She expected them to see her as a woman of strength, courage, and pride. It was her expectation that these personal characteristics helped to dispel the general misconceptions of some of her employers that her background, race, and history of poverty did not define her. Throughout her forty-plus years she toiled in this profession, all of her employers and their children, regardless of their age, addressed her as "Susie." She felt that her name sounded warm and fuzzy when the children called her "Susie." This didn't bother her because there was never any malice involved. However, when she had those verbal confrontations or disagreements with a couple of her house ladies, she detected an undertone of total disrespect for her as an adult. "I felt hurt, angry, and put down." Tee remembers getting so upset she retreated to her room. She didn't care about getting fired because she knew she could find another job. She went back downstairs and told her employer that "slavery was over and she will never allow anyone to talk to her in that manner." The employer apologized for her mean words and promised not to hurt her again. Tee was not fired. Except for the Cokells Tee was older than all her employers, who are now deceased.

According to Tee, there were nights after a long day filled with numerous chores when she felt tired, lonely, and unhappy with the boring circumstances of her life. She thought that perhaps these episodic periods of despair were the result of her carrying, for years, the emotional and financial burden of her large, struggling family. The courage to roll out of bed each morning, still tired from yesterday's work load, was refueled when she reflected on how many individuals had benefited from her hard work.

CHAPTER 5

THE EXODUS FROM THE SOUTH

They came by train, bus, and automobile.

By the middle of 1930, Tee and Willie Bennett, one of her schoolmates, had rented a small apartment in Harlem. This was a place for the ladies to go on their days off from their sleep-in jobs, usually on Thursdays and every other Sunday. It also served as the temporary living quarters where family and friends from the south stayed while looking for work and their own apartment. Later, this apartment was the headquarters where Calhoun School Alumni met to network and strengthen old bonds.

The country was in the throes of the Great Depression 1936 when Tee encouraged my mother, Bettie, to come to New York to take a job as a domestic housekeeper. My father and the other farmers had been out of work for months and no possibility of finding work in the near future. At that time my parents had three young children and agonized over their options—accept the job, or stay home and care for her children. My mother accepted the job, weaned her nine-month-old baby Georgia, leaving Doris and me in the care of my father and our two grandparents. My mother worked on the job for ten months and returned home. She said that she hated the work and she missed her children. My father always interjected that she was lonely for him.

Tee had sent for her two sisters Verbena and Eva a few years earlier to see if they wanted to work and live in New York.

Verbena worked for a few months, returned home, married, and started her family. Eva found a job in a laundry and cleaning establishment in Mt. Vernon. She loved New York and made it her permanent home.

During these years, there was a massive departure of people from the farming towns and cities in the south, which seemed to have been hit the hardest by the Great Depression. Farmers and many other unemployed citizens turned to their government for surplus food to sustain them during this perilous period in our history. Tee received numerous requests from relatives from the south asking for money and a place to stay until they found employment. She did what she could, but the list of individuals making requests was more than she could handle. Fortunately, she was still employed by the wealthy Cokells, had a steady income, and was not in jeopardy of losing her job.

In the spring of 1945, Tee received a letter from a cousin that she had never met. The young lady lived in Kentucky, had just graduated from high school and desperately wanted to come to New York. Her uncle, who was also her guardian, encouraged her to write to his cousin Susannah for permission to come live with her in New York until she could get on her feet. Thrilled to receive a positive response from Tee, her cousin Maggie, whom we call Mac, soon arrived in New York. Mac lived in the ladies' Harlem apartment until she secured a job and her own apartment. Mac developed a close relationship with Tee, who provided support and guidance to Mac during her young adult life. Tee also played a significant role in helping Mac to raise her daughter Valerie. The two are still very close to Tee and currently play a role in her care.

Mac was among the first group of young ladies of her generation that Tee assisted in coming north. Daisy Mae, another cousin, arrived a little later, but didn't stay more than a couple of years before returning home to Alabama.

While most of the young people from the south looking for temporary living quarters and jobs were females, there were some male relatives who needed a supportive networking system to tell them where the jobs were located. Tee's three male cousins; Tommy, Frank and Penn, individually came north and found jobs and housing without any help from relatives. This nomadic lifestyle was not unusual for males, but uncommon for females.

Back during the thirties and forties, young ladies who had graduated from high school, or reached early adulthood, couldn't just pack a bag and leave home and not tell their parents where they were going. They had to have an address and the name of someone their parents knew. Young adult men though were not required to adhere to such rules. They were known to take off on their own, or sometimes with a buddy, and disappear. They didn't necessarily need any money, or even a prearranged place to stay. With a few personal items and something to eat, the males hopped on the first freight train passing through their little towns and cities. They would hobo from one city to another. When they reached their destination, or a city they liked, they found a job and settled down. Hoboing was a very popular method of traveling during that period because jobs and money were scarce. It has since been outlawed, but occasionally men, and now women, can be seen hoboing, carrying on the tradition.

Tee sent for me after I graduated from high school in 1951. The last time I'd seen my aunt was 1946, when she came home to visit. I really didn't know her. I went to live and work with her as a mother's helper for about eight months while she was still with the Andrews. During those months, I bonded with Tee and observed up close how hard she worked and how strong she was physically and emotionally. Sometimes her job required her to be on her feet from early morning until late at night. Yet, she was the first one out of bed and on the job early the next morning. I just admired her for her stamina and dedication to whatever causes kept her going each day. I realized years later that Tee's high expectations and hopes for future generations were the major motivational factors that drove her to work so hard. She wanted the next generation in school getting their education and/or job training programs that offered marketable employment skills.

During those few months, I lived with Tee at the Andrews, I remember one Sunday after church she sat me down and asked me what I wanted to do with my life. I told her that I really wanted to go to college and I was hoping to get a job, and perhaps go to school part time to become a physical education teacher. I could tell from the expression on her face that she didn't like my choice of profession. In an effort, I guess to appease her; I added some more positive achievements, such as good grades, about my excelling in various sports and how much I really liked sports and wanted to work with children. I remember that Tee just looked at me but didn't say one word. My feelings were hurt because she apparently was not impressed with my academic performance, which I was proud of, and so were my parents. Tee got up from the bed where she was sitting and pulled from the bureau drawer an envelope and handed it to me. She said, "This is an application for you to apply to college. If you are accepted, I will pay your board and tuition." I jumped up from my chair, grabbed her around the neck, nearly knocking her down, kissing her and thanking her for this special gift. Tee shared that my parents knew but they were asked not to tell me. They were elated and reassured me that I would do well and make everyone proud.

Although I don't remember promising not to disappoint her, in my excitement I must have said something to the effect that she will never regret that she made this sacrifice for me. I don't believe that she gave me a lecture about what not to do when I got to college. What really surprised me was that Tee had already discussed the matter of sending me to college with her minister, Reverend Wilcox, who was an alumnus of the college where she wanted me to go. She trusted him and was pleased with his recommendations that Livingstone College was an appropriate academic setting for me. As it turned out, her minister, who later became my minister, made a good choice. Those four years at Livingstone were among the happiest times in my life.

Tee didn't tell me, but I learned from others in my family that Tee was very disappointed when she could not fulfill her dream of going to college. Because of this missed opportunity she promised to send to college the first female born in the family. We now feel that our aunt's obsession with our going to college was related to her missed opportunity. So, when I graduated from college, Tee had fulfilled her promise and hopefully, a small part of her dream. Over the years, she helped other relatives and young people fulfill their dreams.

As I reflect on Tee's life, her long work history, and her personal sacrifices, I think of a woman who made a selfless decision early in her life to assume a guardianship role for her siblings' children. She knew that none of her siblings were able to financially support and educate their children without some kind of scholarship or other financial assistance. Financial assistance for Negro students during the 1950s was rare but available for exceptionally smart or athletically gifted students. Our cousin, James Glover, called Sonny, a gifted athlete, attended Kentucky State College, was among the few Black students who received scholarships during that time period. Also, there were a number of special scholarships and grants from various organizations and churches. But many of these didn't cover the full cost of a four-year college program. Our parents, nonetheless, cherished education and persisted on pushing and encouraging us to stay in school. Due to their dogged persistence and Tee's support, those who stayed in school had successful careers.

When my siblings and I were in college, our parents didn't have any money to help us out financially. We worked on campus to defray some of the cost of tuition. However, each of us received packages from home on a regular basis with all kinds of special treats from the farm and our mother's kitchen back in Alabama. These packages represented their love, support, and ongoing encouragement. We are so thankful for their sacrifices. Now that we are adults with one and two children, we are amazed our parents successfully raised ten children during a time of strife, poverty, and turmoil in history. We are blessed to have grown up on a farm where we worked too hard to have the fire or energy to get into trouble. How fortunate we were to have had great parents and our faithful Aunt Tee, who functioned like a third wheel throughout our lives.

About a year after I arrived in New York, my next oldest sister, Doris, came north and lived with Aunt Eva in Mt. Vernon. I left the Andrews and shared an apartment with Doris until I left for college in the fall of 1951. While living in Mt. Vernon, Doris and I were supervised by two male cousins, Tommy Sampson and Frank Mushatt. The cousins treated us like we were their daughters, wanting to know where we were at all times. Frank had a car and on weekends took us to the beaches and baseball games at Yankee Stadium and Ebbet Fields. Frank was a Dodgers fan and loved Jackie Robinson. Every time Jackie Robinson played at home, Frank had to go see him play. Sometimes, Frank's wife, Millie, joined us. I remember that Frank was the first person to try to teach us how to drive until I almost wrecked his car. After three months, I left for college. Doris has never forgiven me "for leaving her alone in Mt. Vernon."

With Tee's support and encouragement, Mary Lou, our first cousin from Kentucky came to New York seeking employment soon after I left and became Doris's roommate. She stayed in New York for several months but eventually returned back home to her family. Within a short period of time, Rosetta, another cousin from Kentucky, arrived and later became Doris's running buddy. After a couple of years Rosetta returned home, and joined the Armed Forces.

Since Tee played a role in encouraging all these young ladies to come to New York, she clearly felt responsible for what happened to them. The goal was for them to find jobs, improve their lives, and help their struggling families back home. Tee only offered her nieces and cousin Mac temporary living quarters until they found jobs. Other relatives, in their desperation to leave home, arrived with Tee's address and a few clothes expecting that they had a place to stay. Clearly, they did not understand Tee's living situation, and like many of her close family members, had a false impression of Tee's financial status. Tee's friend Willie, with whom she shared the apartment, also had family and friends who needed some place to stay when they came north.

The parents of the young ladies expected my aunt to look after their daughters, to help them to find some kind of respectable job, and hopefully, a descent husband. This was an awesome responsibility for my aunt who worked full time with very little time off for herself. Eventually some of these young ladies found jobs; others got married and made New York their home. Tee provided the best supervision and guidance she could for these inexperienced, unskilled young ladies. As she said decades later, "I gave everyone I could a chance."

Ironically, Tee didn't encourage any of the young ladies to seek positions as domestic homemakers. Apparently, this was one of those positions she wanted them to avoid. She had done great things with the little money she earned but the work was very hard, sometimes demeaning, and the wages totally inadequate.

She struggled internally to do her job with pride and dignity, re-
alizing that she didn't have much choice at this point in her life.
Blessed with a strong healthy body, good health, and unsinkable
faith in God, she persevered. Sometimes when she felt low and
discouraged, Tee said, "I would spend my week's pay shopping
for my little nieces and nephews, buying clothing and toys for
Christmas and their birthdays. It gave me great joy anticipating
how the children would react when they opened their individually wrapped gifts at Christmastime." My siblings and I clearly
remember receiving those neatly wrapped packages from Tee.
Our packages were never late because Tee mailed them three to
four weeks prior to Christmas. There were always two beautiful
dresses for the girls and two outfits for our brother. The clothes
that Tee sent were saved for church service.

Every year, a few weeks after Christmas, our mother would
help each of us write Tee a thank you letter for the Christmas
presents. Despite her busy work schedule, Tee would write back
to us to let us know how happy she was that we liked what she
had sent us. It was a joy to receive a personal letter from my
favorite Aunt Tee, not only because she was the only one who
wrote us, she always made you feel so very special. As a young
child, it was exciting to receive a letter with your name in Tee's
unique penmanship. She usually began her letters with "My
Dearest Niece" or "my Dearest Nephew." Over the last several
decades, we have tried to return to Tee some of the true love and
affection we feel for all of the magnificent and happy childhood
experiences she brought to our lives.

While Tee scrutinized the young ladies' dates when she could,
she closely guarded her own romantic life, especially from her
family. It has been impossible to engage Tee in a dialogue concerning the men she dated. Even though the man she married was
out of her life long before we arrived, he is still a mystery to us.

Tee never talks about her husband, Mr. Henry Jones. We have never seen pictures of him. Many years ago she revealed that she dated a gentleman when they attended boarding school, but she refuse to divulge his name. We heard from some of her friends that Tee dated two men following her separation from Mr. Jones but no one shared their names with us either.

Tee was from the old school when it was thought to be disrespectful for young people to question their romantic relationships. Nonetheless, she had an opinion about the men her young relatives dated. Just one brief observation and a brief conversation with these guys, and my aunt had made up her mind. "Where did you find that one?" "Get rid of him." Or "He is no good." She once commented that one gentleman had no plans for his future. Another time, she didn't like the way the young man carried himself. "He just looks lazy and sorry." What I think my aunt was trying to tell us was that these guys were not good enough for us. She did not want us to get involved with the wrong guys.

*Tee with Ginger
in California 1938*

*My Mother Bettie and Tee at
my graduation1951*

Tee in California1940

Rose and John Atchison

Tee, Rev. Wilcox and the Greater Centennial AME Church
Alabama Club in Mt. Vernon, NY circa 1950

Tee's Brother Cody with wife
Annie Mae & baby. Brother
George and Nephew Sonny 1938

Tee in California 1939

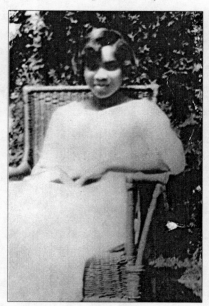

Tee's Sister, Lavilla -1938

George, wife Minnie and
son Hardie

Tee and Lillie in Mexico - 1939

Tee in Belair California 1948

*Tee and Lulabelle in Vermont with
the Andrews children 1952*

CHAPTER 6

THE LADIES' HARLEM APARTMENT

How and from where did all these beautiful, happy,
energetic people come from?

The first time Tee and her friend Maude visited Harlem in 1923; they were surprised when they emerged from their train at 125th Street, in Harlem. It was the first time either of them had seen that many well-dressed, happy looking Black people in one place. At that time, according to an essay "Harlem, A Century in Images" written by Elizabeth Alexander, the Black population in Harlem was 70 percent. By 1950 the population had increased to 98 percent, and by 2008, it had dropped to 62 percent.

Harlem became a Black neighborhood during the early 1900s, starting with the purchase of a large block of houses by a Black realtor and a church group. Black people gradually purchased or rented apartments in the upper part of Harlem several blocks uptown from the busy shopping and entertainment area. When Tee and her friends decided that they needed a place to go on their days off, they chose an apartment uptown.

My aunt and many of her friends arrived in New York during a period known as the Harlem Renaissance, between the 1920s and 1930s. It was a cultural movement and probably one of the most exciting periods for "Negroes." Many of these individuals came from southern states seeking better standards of living and relief from institutional racism. This period captured the essence of a progressive awaking of a class of citizens who were determined to use their energy to resist the continued denial of their civil rights as American citizens.

This era was also characterized by the 1929 Stock market crash and the beginning of the Great Depression, when a great number of "Negroes" migrated by the hundreds to such cities as Chicago, Philadelphia, Cleveland, Detroit, and New York. Harlem, though, attracted the greatest number of "Negroes" from the south.

For the next couple of decades, between 1930 and 1950, Harlem gradually gained an educated class of people who helped to shape the social, political, and economic landscape of the area. Harlem became a center of culture for the Black middle class and soon attracted people of every race and color from every corner of the world. People came to Harlem for different reasons. Some came to shop in an area where merchants had opened up hundreds of shops and store fronts. Then, there were those who came for the cultural and social life, others for the music and the dancing. Harlem was noted for it night clubs and bars where many Black entertainers got their start in show business and the theatre.

Harlem also attracted artists, writers, and photographers. The residents purchased or built beautiful neighborhood churches, sometimes next door to one of the many small storefront churches. Tee remembered a time when people came to Harlem for inspiration, to feel the pulse, and to draw strength and courage from watching the happy, well-dressed men and women strolling down 125th Street. On weekends, Harlem residents had to compete for walking space on sidewalks because so many visitors flooded the area. They came to shop for fashionable clothes, dine-in restaurants that served ethnic food, to visit popular bars, night clubs, and to listen to live music.

Artist, writers and other professionals were inspired to use their skills and talents to enhance the image and lifestyles of Black people to fight racism and discrimination, especially in the work force and housing. Their combined efforts were instrumental in establishing powerful groups and organizations that promoted Black causes in the wider community. The goal was to pave the way for the next generation of individuals to continue to carry the torch of ongoing progress, to pursue social values, education, religion, and political aspirations. To also encourage the election of political figures that are committed to promoting those issues that are relevant to Black people's life and community.

Unlike some of her friends, Tee didn't go to Harlem for the shopping or the entertainment. She was not a partying person, but if something extraordinarily in Harlem interested her, then she would go there. For instance, she was in Harlem to see Dr. Martin Luther King when he come there for a book signing and sustained a life-threatening injury by a mentally deranged woman.

Whenever Tee wanted to meet some of her friends at their apartment, she took the train from her job in Westchester to 125th Street, where she either took a bus or cab to the apartment. She was attending one of her school's meetings at their apartment when the group learned that the Calhoun Boarding School, where they had gone, was in serious financial trouble. The men and women met several times and founded the Calhoun Club to raise funds to save their school. Calhoun Clubs were organized in all the major northern states. Later the Calhoun Club was changed to The Calhoun School National Alumni Association. The main objectives of the Association were to raise funds to support the school and to provide financial assistance to disadvantaged students with scholarships and loans to pay their college education.

The Calhoun National Alumni Association held its first Alumni Reunion in Detroit, Michigan, in 1957. Tee and her classmates from New York were well represented. Over one hundred men and women from cities and towns across the country were there for this premier meeting. The group pledged their continued support for the Calhoun School as well as student loans and scholarships. At its peak during the 1960s, the Association had over two hundred members on its roster. Tee, one of the founding members, served as president and treasurer. She was an active member for many years. It made her very proud that two members of her family were recipients of college loans from the Association.

After some forty years, of providing loans and scholarships for numerous students, the Calhoun National Alumni Association went out of business. The dedicated members were getting too old and disabled to travel to the meetings. The next generation of Calhoun graduates seemed to lack the interest and enthusiasm for raising funds and sustaining the Calhoun spirit. Additionally, the school became public and with the integration of public schools, students' loans became available. The Association became obsolete. However, the original concept was not only visionary but courageous and timely, as most of the scholarship and loan recipients might not have gone to college. In honor of her years of service to the school, the Harvard University Library Open Collection Program presented Tee a portfolio of prints of the Calhoun Colored School. Tee is the only surviving member of the club founders.

CHAPTER 7

TEE BREAKS HER EIGHTEEN-YEAR HIATUS

The time will come when one has to revisit sounds and sights of the past.

" As my train neared home in Alabama, in 1940, I felt pained seeing the deterioration, and the ravages of time engraved on the landscape. Grim and gloomy as usual in February, I saw abandoned houses, barren fields, bare trees, and an overall sense of neglect and hopelessness. Young men who had gone off to war weren't returning back home, and young women migrated to the towns and cities as soon as they graduated from high school. The new generation left the fields and farms seeking better opportunities in faraway places, leaving the older generation to struggle on." Tee was trying to paint a picture of what she saw and felt on her return to Alabama eighteen years later. Years of toiling on the farm and untreated illnesses had taken their toil on the people. Young, strong men and women in the prime of their lives when she left home in 1922 now looked old and downtrodden. She commented that, "I wasn't sad or sorry for the betterment of the younger generation, but it saddened my heart to see the living situations among some of the older members of my family and their neighbors."

Tee remarked that she didn't know what she expected to see once she arrived back in her neighborhood, "because no one prepared me for what my eyes were showing me." The letters from home, she said, were usually about relatives' health, marriages, births, and the deaths of family and neighbors.

After we were adults, we wanted to know from Tee why it took her so long to come back home to see her family. She tried to explain that the trip was rather expensive and she decided that her family could really use that money. She admitted, though, that she regretted having stayed away so long. "It's tough being so far away from home when someone in the family dies, you have to grieve alone."

While Tee was busy getting reacquainted with her relatives upon her return home, my father Callie was sitting around with his brother George and a couple of his male cousins describing the scene Tee created when she arrived at the train station. He of course embellished some of the details to entertain the guys who loved sitting around sharing jokes. Apparently, the train seldom stopped to take on or discharge passengers at the Calhoun train station, which was where Tee was being discharged. The train usually slowed down and the mail bag was thrown out to the Station Master, who was there to pick it up. The day Tee arrived, the train stopped. Local residents who had come to the train station, which was also a little country store and the post office, stopped what they were doing to see what big celebrity was getting off the train. My father told the fellows that the porter stepped off the train with his step stool and these beautiful pieces of luggage which he handed to the Station Master. The porter then took the hand of this beautifully dressed Colored woman and carefully assisted her down the train steps. He bowed and gave her a warm goodbye smile. The residents, my father said, walked away stunned and gradually returned to their previous activities. Tee was forty years old and had acquired a taste for expensive, tailored clothing. She especially loved hats, and bags which she wore to church, social affairs, and the city. Her arrival in Alabama occurred on a cold day in February, and Tee wore a lovely hat and beautiful wool coat with a huge fur collar.

Tee said the highlight of her trip home was that she witnessed a miracle, "my sister-in-law Bettie gave birth to a beautiful, healthy girl, and I had the honor of naming her Lois Leigh." Now, in her old age, especially if she thinks that Lois is getting fresh with her, Tee reminds Lois in an equately fresh but playful voice, "I was there when you were born, and I knew you before you knew yourself." My sisters Doris, Lois, and Selbra are Tee's earthly angels, watching over her in these declining years. Cousin Mac, and her daughter Valerie, are also helping out with her care.

After Tee returned from visiting her family in Alabama, she received a letter from her sister, Eva, with sad news that her maternal grandmother Cindy had passed. Based on the 1880 Census Records, Cindy was 115 years old when she died in 1940. We remember Great-Grandmother Cindy as being a very frail looking, tall woman who walked around the house that she shared with her daughter Mary, our grandmother. Great-Grandmother Cindy walked with a cane and smoked a pipe. Due to her gaunt appearance, young children were afraid of her and would not go near her.

Six months following the death of her Grandmother Cindy, Tee's mother Mary died, at 65. Tee knew that her mother was ill when she visited her, but didn't expect her to go so soon. "I was so glad that I got home to see my mother and my grandmother before they passed on. I am at peace with that," she said.

CHAPTER 8

THE RETIREMENT YEARS

"It's time to take off this uniform, apron,
support stockings, Oxford shoes and rest my knees."

In 1965, Tee retired after working 45 years as a domestic home-maker and childcare worker. By that time, Robert Watson and I were married and lived in East Elmhurst, Long Island with our two children, Audrey and Russ. Tee came to live with us and cared for our children while we were at work. Even though we paid Tee a salary, we did not want her to do any housework; no cleaning, cooking or doing the laundry, because she was not our housekeeper and those days were gone. Having her live with us was a great joy and a blessing for she nurtured, loved, and gave our children the best care. Tee never questioned our child rearing rules and disciplines.

Audrey and Russ were well-behaved youngsters, but there were times when they disobeyed rules and were disciplined. We usually sat down and talked with them about their behavior and denied them some special privileges for a period of time. I knew when Tee didn't approve of our punishment; she would get up and go to her room as though she was the one being punished. After our children grew up, she confided in me that she couldn't bear to see her children being punished because they were sweet, well behaved, and they never gave her a drop of trouble. During those nine years she lived with us, she never made any remark about how she felt about the way we raised our children.

When Tee learned that Bob and I were expecting our first child, she told us that she wanted to be one of our baby's Godparents. We told her that it would be an honor to give her that honor. When Audrey, our first child was born, Tee scurried on in into Bloomingdale's and purchased this exquisite christening ensemble for her Godchild. Thirty-nine years later, our granddaughter Susannah, Tee's namesake, was christened in the same dress that we are saving for the next females in the family. Tee took her guardianship roles and responsibilities very seriously, providing support, guidance, and love to Audrey all of her life.

My aunt loved and respected my husband, Bob, whom she called Bobby. He was always patient and kind to Tee, who reminded him of his grandmother, Flora Watson, who raised him. I know he was happy to have Tee as part of our family. Tee was impressed with Bob the first time she met him. She told me she "liked his mannerism, his patience, and the way he carried himself." Then she whispered in my ear, "Don't let him get away." Everyone thought that Tee was Bob's aunt because they had such a close, warm relationship.

The only time I can remember Tee making Bob angry was when Tee sneaked and bought Russell another bottle to suck after we agreed that at age three, he no longer needed a bottle. With Russell's knowledge, we had gotten rid of his bottles. Bob came home early from work one day and saw a half bottle of milk on the kitchen counter. When Tee realized that Bob saw the bottle before she could it hide it again, she started apologizing. "Oh, I am so sorry, Bobby, but he was asking for his bottle." So Bob got rid of that bottle too. When we moved from that house four years later, we found another dust-covered bottle on top of the kitchen cabinets. I am sure Russell gave up the bottle before Tee! Years later, when Tee reminds us about that incident, she laughs and then becomes emotional. She is remorsefully remembering a sad time in our lives when we lost Bob in 2002.

Tee loved going grocery shopping with Bob on Saturday mornings. She almost never went grocery shopping with me because she said I had to make too many stops: the drug store, cleaners, shoe shop, post office, and the bakery. By the time we returned home, Tee was exhausted just sitting in the car waiting for me to finish my Saturday chores. When our children were very young, our son Russell went along with his father and Tee, while Audrey became my shopping partner.

When Tee entered the grocery store, she grabbed her own shopping cart. She threw her walking cane in the cart and leaned on the back of the cart as she strolled down each aisle, searching for some special item. During the years she lived us, Tee accumulated a large collection of spices and other ingredients she used when preparing special dishes. She said cooking what she wanted, when she wanted to, gave her the greatest pleasure. Tee and Bob's last stop was at the meat market where Tee assisted Bob in selecting meats for the family. The butcher called her Grandma and was always glad to see her because Tee preferred the more expensive cuts of meat. Bob's knowledge and understanding of different meats and how to prepare them improved under Tee's expert tutelage. Tee was an excellent teacher with the ability to help any novice prepare the most difficult dishes.

During the holidays, Bob always ordered Tee a duck from the butcher, which she prepared, and the two of them ate. Duck meat didn't appeal to other members of the family. Tee seemed pleased to have something special that only she and Robert had in common, their duck, while the rest of the family ate other meats.

Although I prepared most of the family's meals, Bob would occasionally prepare his special meals for the family, especially on weekends. Tee didn't always enjoy or approve of my cooking. As a matter of fact, she could be quite critical of my cooking and did her best to teach me some of the basic culinary and serving skills. I didn't feel the need to explain to Tee that from early morning until late at night, five-days a week, I was a full-time multitasking wife, mom, employee, and sometimes student, who didn't have the time or energy to prepare the family's meal with a lot of love. I must admit that I am a better cook due to Tee's valuable training. Sometimes, Tee surprised the family by preparing one of her special dinners. On many occasions, we would walk through the door and be greeted with a mouth-watering aroma coming from the kitchen, and find Tee happily humming as she prepared one of her favorite dinners. She loved it when we told her how great it smelled and how anxious we were to eat. During these special times, she reminded us how great it felt to be the one being served, and not the server. Tee's favorite dinner was perhaps a lamb roast stuffed with cloves of garlic and other spices, augmented with small red-skinned potatoes, pearl onions, string beans, and some kind of special dessert for the children.

Another family weekend activity that Tee enjoyed immensely was accompanying the family to the plant nursery during the spring. With more time on her hand since both children were in school, she had begun to collect and nurture a number of different plants that she grew on her bedroom window ledges and on the floor in her room. She derived great pleasure growing plants from small cuttings that she just stuck in the soil and nurtured until they grew into big plants. She seemed to have had an affinity for African violets plants, which now come in multiple colors. Tee's bedroom became a small nursery. As Audrey and Russ grew up, and were away all day, those plants symbolically became Tee's "children." She needed something to nurture!

On weekends, holidays, and during the summers when we were home from our jobs with the school system, Tee frequently visited family members and friends in the city. It was during those early years of her retirement when we began to have our family gatherings at one of our homes or apartments to celebrate birthdays, weddings, christenings, and major holidays. These occasions gave the adults an opportunity to see each other and our children to meet and play with their cousins.

We were anxious for our children to develop and maintain those strong family bonds that we as siblings, and cousins established growing up in Alabama. It is our goal to keep these family gatherings alive with the hope that future generations will retain something of value about their culture and our family tradition. Children who know their family's history seem to have more self-confidence, according to psychologist Dr. Marshall Duke at Emory University and his colleague Dr. Robin Fivush. The researchers found that, "The ones who knew a lot about their families tend to do better when they face challenges." A strong "intergenerational self," it appears, helps children to know that they belong to something bigger than themselves.

When our families meet, we share stories relevant to our parents, grandparents, and other relatives. We talk about hard times, happy and sad times, and how we pulled through as a family. Our children need to know that they belong to a group of people who love and care about them. When our parents were still alive, we often piled the children in two cars and took them to our farm in Alabama, where they ran wild for two weeks during the summer. Supervising a half dozen young, active youngsters was a huge responsibility on our parents, especially our mother, who assumed a more active role, cooking, cleaning, and doing loads of laundry every day. Spending summers with his grandchildren was a fun time for our father. He looked forward to piling all the children in the back of his truck, driving them to the store to buy them junk food. The children cherish those summers and talk about those memorable times whenever they get together.

For our family gatherings, everyone except Tee brings one or two special dishes. Tee, religiously chooses her favorite corner in the kitchen and asks for "a little taste" of every dish that comes through the door. Every once in a while she makes a comment about some ingredients being omitted, or that a certain meat was over-cooked. She loved interjecting her comments about how the food was prepared, how we should do it the next time.

When the food is ready, someone prepares Tee a man's size dish. Tee can be heard in the background ordering whoever is preparing her dish, "Remember, I want a sampling of all the dishes." She always praised the cooks "for making all this delicious food," and thanked the host family for inviting everyone to their home. We could never understand how a woman of Tee's stature and age could consume so much food and never get sick. Clearly, our aunt enjoyed these occasions more than anyone. She is now the matriarch of six generations of Mushatts. For those who didn't know Tee well, it was a chance to meet and love this wonderful, generous, dependable woman we called "Tee." We couldn't do enough for this devoted woman with the big, dependable shoulders that so many had climbed on and changed the direction of their lives.

One beautiful spring afternoon ten years after Tee moved in with us, she pulled me from the door before I had a chance to set down my briefcase. "I need to talk with you about something," she said. Immediately, my mind scurried across dire possibilities. Was she ill? Had someone in the family died? She looked at me and softly told me, "I want to go home." I took a hard look at her, trying to understand what she was talking about, because Robert and I were under the impression that our house was her home. Then she clarified that she wanted to go to Alabama to be near her two brothers, Callie and George. When I found my voice, I asked her what happened, wasn't she happy with us? Tee could see that I was getting emotional when she grabbed me by the shoulders and said, "You know better than that; these years have been the happiest times in my life." I commented that probably she just needed to go spend a few months with her brothers, she would feel better; she could come back home and stay with us when she was ready. Tee then gave me that talk about not having anything to do now that the children were away all day, and she lived so far from her family and friends. While all of that was true, I thought that my aunt liked the idea of visiting with relatives and friends in the city. In the past, whenever she wanted to go into the city one of us would drive her, or my brother Callie would come to get her. I could tell that Tee had been thinking about this decision for a while. She had made up her mind.

Through tears, I tried to tell my aunt what a pleasure it had been to have her live with us, and how thankful and blessed Bob and felt to have her play such an important role in the young lives of Audrey and Russ. The thought of not having Tee around, after all those years, was just painful to think about.

Tee was worried about how she was going to tell Bob and the children about her decision to live in Alabama. She asked what I thought she should tell them. She said that she didn't want to hurt her children and she surely didn't want Bob to get the impression that she wasn't grateful to him for welcoming her into his home. I reassured her that Bob would understand and she had to tell the children the truth. I had already shared with Bob the sad news of Tee's decision when she made the announcement one day after dinner. The children wanted to know when she would return home. Sadness swept over their faces when they realized that Tee would not be returning home to live with us. Bob softened their shock by saying that Tee was always welcome to come back. I promised to take them south to see Tee and their grandparents during the summers when school was out.

At the end of the school year in1975, we drove my seventy-five-year-old aunt to Alabama to live with my parents. Tee was excited seeing relatives and old friends in the community. Many of her old classmates and friends had passed on, or were unable to participate in the kinds of social activities that Tee still enjoyed. Aunt Tee soon became our mother's companion, traveling with her on various trips to visit the sick, grocery shopping, and church. She joined the Senior Center, where she enjoyed socializing and participating in the arts and crafts program two or three times a week. We had mixed feeling about leaving Tee in Alabama. We wanted her to be happy, but we were concerned she was going to live in a different environment completely from the one she'd known. I was also worried that Tee would miss her friends back in New York.

Within a year of moving to Alabama, Tee decided she wanted her own place. She purchased a two bed-bedroom mobile home, which she placed on the edge of my parents' yard. She was close enough to sit on her porch and have a conversation with my parents on their porch. Tee enjoyed my mother's cooking and sometimes joined them at mealtime when she didn't want to cook. When we went home to visit the family, Tee was encouraged to join us for most of her meals. Tee especially enjoyed watching the little ones run back and forth between the two houses. Uncle George and his family lived close by and visited with his siblings regularly. The highlight of our visit home was at breakfast when our mother treated everyone to her popular breakfast; homemade biscuits, sausage, grits with pear and peach preserves. The preserves were made by my mother from peaches and pears from our orchards.

Tee stayed in touch with her friends back north—Willie Bennett, Viola Taylor, Elliot and Nelly McCray, and Bernice Morton. She missed her friends and their monthly Calhoun

Alumni meetings. They were hoping that Tee would return to New York.

Valerie, Tee's Godchild asked her one day if she was ready to return to New York. Tee told her no, but later changed her mind. This period of ambivalence was a difficult time for Tee because there were a series of issues she had to consider. If she came back to New York, was she ready and prepared to live in the city alone at this stage of her life, or would she prefer to live with one of her relatives. But where? Although Robert and I still lived on Long Island, she felt this was too far away from the city where most of her friends lived.

It took Tee two months to finally make a decision about where she wanted to live. She never discussed with anyone what issues she considered when she made the decision to finally return to New York after living in Alabama for five years. Although it broke my father's heart when Tee announced that she was returning to New York, he was not as upset as he was back in 1922, when she left home. I think that it relieved my parents to know that when Tee returned to New York, their children would look after her. Her leaving in many ways, removed a burden from them, for they were beginning to have some medical issues themselves.

Upon her return north, Tee resumed her pattern of living with different relatives and visiting with friends throughout the five boroughs. It gave her great pleasure, getting acquainted with the next generation of youngsters born during her absence. Cuddling and rocking the babies and toddlers was like a shot of adrenaline that lifted Tee's spirit. She lets everyone know that she doesn't like to be around too many old people. She didn't care who heard her when she said, "You see, old people can't do anything for you because they have their own health problems, and sometimes they are not nice to be around." Then she adds, "But I love to be around young people, especially the babies." It occurred to a couple of us that there weren't any young babies around Tee when she lived in Alabama. Among other things, she missed living in New York where the young generation, and most of her friends lived.

Living in different homes and the apartments of relatives and friends took its toll on my aunt, who was almost eighty years old. Although she was still in good health and could get around very well, the excitement of returning home had worn off and she was physically tired. There came a time when Tee decided that she wanted a place she could call home, a place close to family and friends, but her own home. With the assistance and recommendations of her of her Goddaughter, Valerie Tee moved into a one-bedroom apartment in the Vandalia Senior Center Housing Development in Brooklyn, where four nieces, two cousins, and many friends lived. The senior citizen apartment is located in a development consisting of a massive complex of buildings; condos, apartments, schools, post office, supermarkets, drug stores, and a host of other amenities. Tee was very pleased with her apartment, which had a lovely front view within walking distance of everything she needed. When she needed to travel, someone in the family drove her. While public transportation was available, Tee never had to use it. We think that our aunt adjusted well to the change and everyone was happy and pleased to have her back in New York.

For some reason, when Tee returned to New York she decided that she didn't want the responsibility of handling her personal affairs such as paying bills, keeping track of medical appointments, and shopping for her clothes and food. She began distributing or assigning specific responsibilities to each of her nieces. Realistically, two people could have handled Tee's affairs, but she was demanding the involvement of everyone. This plan necessitated our spending unnecessary hours on the phone communicating with each other about issues concerning Tee. I am sure Tee's motives were to keep us involved with her life. But having a dozen or more individuals involved in the affairs of one person creates confusion and "bad blood."

It was not unusual for Tee to call her nieces, Georgia and Margie in Alabama, for example, to ask them to send her two pairs of white socks because her doctor didn't want her to wear dark-colored socks and stockings any more. If there was a need for something medical, she called Doris, the nurse. If Tee developed a craving for a certain kind of meat, she was on the phone with Selbra to bring her that particular cut of meat. Tee worried Mac to find her a couple of nice dresses at Bloomingdales that she could wear to club meetings and family gatherings. She had everyone looking for her favorite teas, golden seal and sassafras, which Tee maintained were the best teas because they were medicinal.

Tee is a generous woman who often gives other people lavish gifts. She rarely purchases expensive gifts for herself. Undergarments are the exception. My aunt loves fancy, expensive undergarments. As she grew older and became incontinent, she wore her fancy underpants over her Depends. When it's time to replace her undergarments, she never forgets to say, "Remember, I don't care how much they cost, I want the lacy underpants and slips." I remember Tee calling me one day to ask me to find her a few all-cotton baby washcloths. "Don't ask me why," she said. "Just find them." It was a strange request until I talked with Lois, who was also searching for washcloths. She told me that Tee had developed arthritis in her hands and didn't have the strength to squeeze water from the adult cloths. So our aunt had the two of us searching all over trying to find them.

When we thought about our aunt's demands and weird requests, we realized that she didn't have any experience managing a budget or paying household expenses. Actually, she never had household expenses as a sleep-in domestic homemaker. I know she had an account at Bloomingdale's but that was closed when she moved to Alabama. She paid cash for everything she purchased in recent years. Managing a household budget was not on her list of personal responsibilities she wanted to assume at this stage of her life.

For her eightieth birthday, the family gave Tee a welcome back home/birthday backyard party at our home on Long Island. We invited schoolmates, family, and friends. The party was not a surprise because we needed Tee's help locating these people. At that time several classmates and close friends were alive. Food was prepared and served by the family. Although Tee requested no gifts because, "I have everything I need and want. I just wish everyone who is able will come to my first birthday party."

Of course, when it came to the gifts issue no one listened. Tee received a generous amount of cash. The party was a huge success, and it made Tee feel so happy and proud that everyone who was invited showed up. She thanked everyone for their attendance and for their gifts. She also wanted everyone to know that she was "one blessed, happy woman."

Sometime after her eightieth birthday, Tee seemed bored and was seeking something useful to do with her time that she would enjoy. She continued to enjoy good health, was alert and able to take care of herself. Although she was now using a walking cane, she was able to get around. Tee decided to join the Center Tenant Patrol in her building. Since she loved meeting and talking with people, this seemed to be an ideal way to spend her time and make a contribution. With her vibrant personality and warm greetings, she became a favorite among the tenants and visitors as she welcomed them with a clear, friendly request to "please sign the guest book." Tee sat on Tenant Patrol every day except

Sunday, never missing a day, once in the morning and again after lunch. It's a position that she held for twenty-one years, never missing a day. She was the oldest and most active member on the Tenant Patrol. She said that she enjoyed this position because it gave her an opportunity to meet and talk with different people. A reporter from the New York Times called her "The Intrepi Guardian of Vandalia Housing" because she was not afraid to ask people to sign the guest book.

As Tee approached her ninetieth birthday we observed a gradual change in her mobility. She was obviously slowing down and more dependent on her cane, keeping it near her at all times. There was also less interest and desire to visit with family and friends. However, our aunt was still in good health, eating and sleeping well and was not complaining of pain. However, Tee's eyesight was failing and there is some hearing loss. These physical conditions have been observed by family members who see her frequently and medically confirmed by her doctors. Tee spends a lot of time on the phone usually with family members. She has assigned some members of the family, children included, days when they are to call her. If for some reason one of us forgot to call her on our day, Tee gets on the phone the next day with an insulting voice. "And where were you yesterday?" "You forgot to call me." If we called her a day early, she would promptly tell us it wasn't our day. We were surprised that Tee remembered which day each person was scheduled to call her. Before her friends Willie and Bernice passed, they talked to each other three or four times a day. As Tee's circle of friends dwindled, she had a greater need to hear the voice of someone in her family every day. Tee loves when the weekend comes because that's the day her family visits with her home-cooked southern style meal. These visits are very meaningful to Tee because she enjoys having her family around her.

CHAPTER 9

TEE GIVES HERSELF A BIRTHDAY PARTY

There is no sin in pampering yourself.

A few months prior to her ninetieth birthday, Tee announced to the family she was going to give herself a birthday party. She was going to pay for it but wanted the family to do all the preparation and serving. The party was at our brother Callie Jr. and his wife Jeannette's home in the Bronx. A great number of family and friends from New York and out of town showed up, including our parents, Callie and Bettie Mushatt from Alabama, Tee's cousin Tommie Sampson from Virginia, our mother's brother, Roosevelt Brown from Alabama, Ruth Lembeck and her son, Peter from Westchester. Despite a hot, steamy day in July 1989, everyone had a glorious time, and "The Birthday Lady" was very pleased.

In addition to the elaborate parties given by Tee's family, the Senior Center also celebrates her birthdays with lovely parties in their dinning room. Sometimes, they include other seniors who have birthdays close to Tee's. The Center's staff, and other ladies of the center, serve the guests food and provide music for dancing. In addition to family and friends, noted public officials show up at these parties to present proclamations and other congratulatory plaques to Tee in recognition of her of her long life and her contribution to the center and community. The walls in her apartment are lined with family photos, plaques, letters, and accommodations from presidents, mayors, congressmen, legislators, and other dignitaries.

Remarkably, our aunt Tee has enjoyed an extremely long stage of what gerontologists call "old-old age." She has been chronologically old for a long time, but she didn't look, behave, or feel like most individuals her age. Her medical history is unbelievable considering the fact that she has never been sick enough to be hospitalized. She does have arthritis and was medicating herself with daily doses of aspirin until her doctor asked her to stop taking them. However, Tee refused to give them up, but had to when she couldn't get to the store and couldn't get anyone to get them for her. She maintained that Dr. Landau, her first doctor in Bronxville, New York, advised her to take an aspirin daily. He convinced her that aspirin was one of those miracle drugs, good for almost any pain.

Tee currently takes one medication for hypertension, and daily supplements of iron and vitamin D. She seldom has a cold, and when she does, is able to recover rather quickly due, she says, to the good food she eats and those teas she drinks. She had a hysterectomy during her early fifties and is currently being treated at home for ulcerated wounds on her legs. Perhaps the reoccurring wounds are due to poor circulation, and from standing on her feet so many years. Many years ago when she started to have difficulty with her legs, she was told by her doctor to wear support stockings. Effective treatment for varicose veins was not as available then as it is today. I suspect Tee would not have agreed to have surgery on her legs then or ever. As a young woman, Tee developed pyorrhea of the gums, probably from lack of early dental care, and had to have all of her teeth removed before she was fifty.

Except when she is having one of her tantrums due to

frustration and anger, Tee is a happy, witty woman with an infectious laugh. She can laugh at herself and enjoys a good joke. Her current life is for the most part stress free. That's because she no longer is privy to family problems and emergencies and, because of her hearing loss and blindness, is not directly affected by problems of the world. This calm, relaxed state of existence has reduced our aunt's blood pressure.

I remember when Tee began to have difficulties with her eyes. The ophthalmologist recommended surgery to improve her vision. The doctor was a very gentle middle aged man who explained the procedure to Tee. She never said a word or asked a question. Finally she said that she needed to discuss his recommendations with her family, which she did. As a matter of fact, one of her nieces was with her. Again, our aunt said no surgery.

Sometime during the late nineties, one of Tee's doctors told her that she needed a pacemaker to improve her heart rate, which was too low. She said that she would discuss it with her family and let him know what they thought about his recommendations. Tee's instructions to us was, "Don't ever give anyone permission to cut my body." She looked around at the family members who were present to make sure that everyone heard her. "Did everyone hear me?" "No surgery on any part of my body." Everyone agreed to abide by her wishes, and we will. Tee's doctor was furious with the family, convinced that we encouraged her not to have the surgery. My sister Lois found Tee another doctor who has never told the family that Tee needed a pacemaker. Tee's slow-beating heart has been beating just fine for the last six years.

We realized that our aunt was getting up in age and would eventually develop some health issues. We felt she needed a health proxy on file with her doctors. The term "proxy" was foreign to her, but once she understood the meaning and implication, she thought it was a good idea, but said, "I want the family to decide what should happen to me. I don't want to be hooked up to those machines, I am old and I have lived a good long life." Tee sat back in her chair, closed her eyes and said, "Now, I want all of you to agree to my wishes, but I will not sign that proxy unless everyone signs it. Because of Tee's unwillingness to adhere to the terms of the proxy, we decided this was not an issue we needed to fight with her about.

Tee is very stubborn once she makes up her mind she doesn't want to do something, particularly when it involves her body, which she has control over. She intends to die with her body intact. I remember when Tee began having difficulties with her eyes and the ophthalmologist recommended cataract surgery that would improve her vision. Despite a gentle conversation about the procedure, a month to discuss it with family, which she did, Tee was unrelenting in her decision not to have surgery on her eyes. The explanation she gave us was that she had lost most of the vision in one eye already (her doctor knew this), resulting from a childhood injury. She wasn't going to take a chance having surgery on her good eye. Sadly, she went blind within a short period. Tee handled the loss of her vision very well initially, and we praised her for having such an accepting attitude.

We have diligently struggled over the years to understand, negotiate and pacify our aunt Tee to make her remaining years less stressful and more enjoyable for the sake of everyone. Sometimes, her family goes to the extreme to shine a little light of love and compassion on her current world of darkness and loneliness. Yet, when the family suggests or recommends services, medical procedures, or other plans to improve her overall quality of life, our aunt draws a line in the sand, puts her foot down, and behaves like a stubborn toddler. We are wondering if this mulish behavior is due to fear, lack of trust, or just our aunt's need to hold to some degree of control.

I am thinking about an unusual occurrence when Tee was ninety-five years old. One of my sisters saw Tee yawn and was stunned to see a solitary bottom tooth. Tee knew it was there, yet never said a word. She didn't want it removed. The tooth hooked lonely sitting there all by itself. Initially, the idea of a woman "growing a tooth." at nearly a hundred years old, was hilarious. After a few months, the tooth began to turn yellow. Tee resisted the idea of going to the dentist to have the tooth extracted. She was adamant about keeping her tooth until we convinced her that the tooth was not healthy and may give her trouble in the near future. She finally got the point and the tooth was extracted.

In 2010, we enrolled Tee in The New England Centenarian Study located in Boston. The purpose of the study is to provide researchers an opportunity to identify "rare genes" that protect against diseases, while giving valuable clues to health and longevity. Their method of data collection is simple and noninvasive. Tee agreed to participate in this study after Lois told her what was involved. The first request for data included samples of Tee's blood, hair, and saliva. Lois, a gentle soul when dealing with her aunt, approached her to secure the samples with the nurse and doctor from the study. The doctor and the nurse tried to find a vein to draw blood, but were unsuccessful. Tee remarked at that time, "Never again will I let anyone stick me." Lois had to make two visits before she secured a salvia sample. Each time she went to Tee's apartment to get the salvia, Tee, as usual, was chewing gum. The researchers wanted the sample free of food and gum residue. Tee told Lois "the gum secreted saliva; without the gum, I have no spit for you." Lois said ok and sent the salvia sample to the researchers laced with the flavor of Double Mint chewing gum!

We'd known for some time it would be difficult for Tee to give up some of her independence and accept help with some of her daily care activities, such as cooking , housecleaning, and laundering. By the time she reached her 100th birthday, she was blind and could no longer pretend she could see. Months later, she shared that she found her way to the bathroom at night by tying a string from her bed to the bathroom door. Before she came up with this little arrangement, she would get up some nights to go to the bathroom and get lost in her little three-room apartment. "Those were the nights I cried, all night." She said, "I was feeling lost, helpless and alone, and now I can't take care of myself." It was during this period when we began to see glimpses of Tee's growing vulnerability.

Our aunt gave up the first layer of her pride and accepted home care. In an authoritative voice: "It had better be someone that I like, or I am not keeping her." She found something to complain about with every home care giver the agency sent to her. My aunt's strongest resistance fixated on her dislike for the care givers' "style" of cooking, or she couldn't understand their language. If a woman arrived at her door that she decided she didn't want or like, Tee created havoc, refusing to eat the food the woman prepared, would not communicate with her, and at other times refused to get out bed. Each time Tee acted out, one and sometimes two nieces rushed to her apartment to calm her down and stay with her until another home care giver arrived.

Finally, the home care agency, which has been extremely cooperative and understanding of Tee's behavior and her special needs, found a compatible team of women that Tee likes. Cicely, Tee's current full-time care giver has been with her for ten years. Tee is fond of Cicely, who gives her good care and doesn't tolerate Tee's manipulative behavior. Tee speaks highly of Velma, a gentle woman who cares for Tee when Cicely is off or goes on vacation.

Tee's family commends the Home Care Association of New

York State, Inc. and The Visiting Nurse Association of Brooklyn for high quality of care and supervision provided to our Aunt Tee over the last fifteen years. We strongly support and encourage these agencies' continued commitment to provide care and medical treatment to homebound patients. We believe that the superior home care and medical services the agencies and their staff have provided made it possible for our aunt to remain in her comfortable, familiar apartment. Moreover, living in the neighborhood close to family and friends has enhanced our aunt's quality of life enormously.

For Tee's centennial birthday, we met again at my brother Callie JR. and Jeannette's home for the milestone celebration. A huge number of relatives and friends came to see and talk with a woman who lived to be 100. To some it was a miracle, but to others a blessing. It was one of those rare, perfect July days and Tee was in a good mood and greeted her guests with hugs and kisses. Her large collection of cards, letters, commendations, and proclamations from distinguished dignitaries were read. Among some of her letters included a greeting from President Barack Obama and his wife, Michelle, which states "For over a century you have witnessed great milestones in our Nation's history; your life represents a piece of the American story." New York City Housing Chairman, Tino Hernandez, described Tee as "a model of joy and vitality to your fellow residents and all New Yorkers" in a letter commemorating her 100th birthday. Tee's picture and stories about her life were featured on television and in the local news papers.

A few of the older guests who were present at Tee's ninetieth birthday party were absent this time due to poor health or death. Our aunt was in high spirits and looked well rested and happy in one of her beautiful summer dresses. She was just delighted to meet and hold the two youngest great-grand nieces in the family, three-week-old Nia Lois Mays and five-month-old Susannah Brooke Watson. The family and guests socialized and feasted on a delicious smorgasbord of homemade food. Some of the guests' dishes were prepared by Callie and Jeannette's son, Callie III. Their son Tyrone entertained us with lovely dancing music.

Following Tee's appearance on television, there were several requests for visits from a number of individuals locally and nationally who wanted to interview and or just meet her. Interestingly, some of the people found it hard to believe that a woman who had reached 100 could be alert and have a coherent dialogue about her life. For obvious reasons, most of the requests were denied. However, there were two persistent individuals who were granted short visits with Tee, after Lois met with them. One of the individuals was a priest from Alabama. Father Anthony met with Lois, who was impressed with his sincerity. He talked briefly with Tee, prayed with her, and left. Father Anthony has visited Tee yearly, when he comes to New York to visit his family. Tee likes that he holds her hands when he prays for her.

Elaine McGrowder, the other accepted visitor, an advocate for senior citizens, lives on Long Island. Ms. McGrowder, a trained public health nurse from England was not only persistent in her desire to meet Tee; her broad knowledge of seniors was impressive. She enjoyed talking with Tee, loved her spirit and physical stamina. She has kept in touch with Tee for the last four years.

Tee was wheelchair bound and had to be pushed everywhere she went when we celebrated her 100th birthday. Her knees had given out. She was still alert, recognized familiar voices, and remembered the names of family and close friends. She lost some hearing, which makes phone conversations difficult. Tee claims that her hearing aids are too much trouble, and she refuses to wear them. We noticed during this period she seldom listened to the television or radio. Even after she lost her sight she still listened to reruns of her favorite programs "I love Lucy," "As the World Turns," "Days of Our Lives," and "Wheel of Fortune," rather than some of the new programs. Sometimes, Tee kept her radio on all night tuned to WINS News 24-7 with Paul Harvey, her favorite newsman. Tee's interest in these programs gradually diminished with the loss of her hearing and eyesight. I suspect she became bored with them after so many reruns.

Our Aunt Tee still has a hearty appetite and eats well, but she is beginning to look thin. She's lost some body fat and muscle tone, and looks frail and old. Nonetheless, her voice is strong and she feels physically well. The best part of the day for Tee is mealtime as she loves to eat. Her care givers get her up around nine each morning and prepare a hearty breakfast of bacon, scrambled eggs, toast, and juice. Sometimes she has grits, pancakes, or waffles. Tee has her heaviest meal at lunch. This meal may include a protein such as turkey, lamb stew, chicken, roast beef, meat loaf, or corn beef served with two vegetables. Tee likes all of these vegetables: cabbage, collards, turnips, kale, mustards, corn, and okra. She likes cornbread with her greens. Tee will have mashed potatoes or rice with some of the meats, but she loves sweet potatoes. Jell-O and perhaps cookies are among the desserts she eats regularly, but she loves home cakes and fruit pies.

If Tee doesn't have visitors, after her lunch, she may ask her care giver to put her to bed for her afternoon nap or she may decide to nap in her lounge chair. Her care givers leave the decision up to Tee. They know that it makes everyone's life easier if Tee is allowed to make some decisions for herself. For dinner, Tee eats a lighter meal, sometimes consisting of some of the same foods she had for lunch. Bedtime is around seven or eight. Tee's sleep pattern is becoming sporadic, and if she has a bad night she may want to sleep a little longer in the morning.

Our aunt has lost interest in going out of her apartment to interact with other tenants. Now her excursions are doctor's appointments, which she complains about, and trips to family members' homes for special occasions. She prefers family visits in the comfort of her apartment. The physical requirements involved in traveling are too hard on her, so she avoids going out. My sisters start to prepare Tee for her doctor's appointments a day before they are scheduled, including an explanation of what to expect at the doctor's office and why it's necessary for her to behave and cooperate. They get her to promise not to embarrass them in public by acting out and swearing. Sometimes this plan works, but there are times Tee breaks her promise. She seems to feel that because she is old, she can say and do anything she wishes.

Tee's doctors try to see her as soon as she arrives so that she doesn't have to wait very long. They aren't offended by her occasional abrasive behavior. The doctors and nurses are very fond of our aunt and think she's hilarious, especially when she accuses the male doctors of trying to look under her dress. As their oldest living patient, Tee is everyone's "Darling" in the New York City Health Care System. They know she has a team of diligent advocators supervising her health care to make sure she gets the best medical care the system has to offer its oldest resident.

Our aunt has always been a woman with high standards; dress appropriately, no swearing, respect the elderly, watch your table manners, hold your head up high, and for God's sake, walk properly. So, we were shocked when this gracious woman started swearing in the presence of three nieces, including a young child. Everyone in the car remembers. We were returning home to Brooklyn from a family gathering at our brother's home. All the way home, about forty-five minutes, on a heavily traveled parkway, at night, our aunt, sitting in the front passenger's seat, couldn't resist grabbing the center drive gear. I told her how dangerous that was and asked her not to touch it. She lashed out at me "I hate this damn car, and I'll be glad when I get home." We glanced at each other with that questionable look, "Did you hear what I heard?"

The next day, we casually mentioned the incident to our aunt. She vehemently denied ever using such language, "You know I don't curse, I have never used bad language, it was not allowed when I was growing up." As we thought about Tee's behavior in the car, we concluded that it had been a long day for our aunt. She'd missed her afternoon nap and was probably very tired. Tee's swearing has not only escalated over the years, the language is becoming more colorful, more hilarious, and so out of character for the Tee we know. Tee has lived a semi "sheltered" life, having spent most of her time in the company of children. Where, we wondered, did she learn this language? Foul language was forbidden in her parents' home, certainly not in boarding school, for during that period, her male schoolmates and friends were gentlemen in the presence of their lady friends. It's fruitless to ask Tee about the origin of her language, because we'll only hear a blunt denial.

Jeannette, Little, Callie, Callie II, Delouris and Tyrone

81

Grandniece Chandra sitting with Tee at 100th Birthday party

Callie's daughter, Delouris, husband, Tony and son Christopher

Tee and her neices and cousins Dolla, Mac. Val. Esther, Doris, Bettie, Shawn and Sebra - 1998

Pam,Leah and Henry - 1998

Tee's sister, Verbena, grandchildren and great-grandchildren

Susannah's 107th Birthday Celebration - 2006

Audrey and Darryl (Easter Dinner) 1995

Shirley, Donald and Dolla

Tee with grand and great-grand nieces and nephews

Verbena and Children

Uncle George's children and grandchildren - 2007

Tee's niece Margie and husband George

Tee's schoolmate and friend,
Bernice Morton "Pete" - 2008

Russ and Amber's families,
Sharrits, Leobolds, Rehm and Watsons

Tee's cousin Buck and his wife Earline, Marion and Callie - 1998

Tee's Schoolmates Celebrate her 80th Birthday

*Tee's cousin Selbra on left
and her niece Selbra on the
right at Tee's 80th birthday*

*Russ and Amber Watson
Sept. 17, 2013*

*Susannah's 111th Birthday celebration here with her
grand-niece, Myra 2010*

Tee Celebrates her 80th birthday with schoolmates Willie, Nettie, Ruth, and Mac

Joanne, Barbara, Dolla and Shirley - Oct. 1998

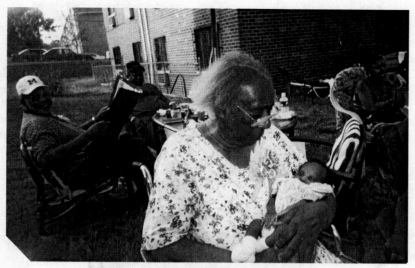

*Tee, the oldest on her 100th birthday,
holding the youngest, Nia Mays*

*John, Lecettie and Doris at Tee's 110th birthday party
at Callie's house, Bronx, NY*

My Parents and Aunt Nancy

Aunt Verbena's children and grandchildren

The Andrews visit Tee
Lois, Carole, Val, Joan, Mac, Audrey, Gail and Paul - 2001

Callie and Jeannette with grandson Christopher

Tee's nephew Greg and family
Liz, Nicole and Michell

CHAPTER 10
THE SUPER CENTENARIAN

New York's oldest living person. She can't believe it!

In July 2009, Tee celebrated another milestone. She joined an elite group of individuals who have reached the 110th year mark – Super Centenarians. This group is also known as the 110 Club. To be declared a Super Centenarian, individuals must be validated by an international body that specifically deals in longevity research, such as the Gerontology Research Group in Atlanta, Georgia. They must submit three documents supporting the age claimed. All the required documents verifying Tee's age were submitted to the Research Group, and according to Dr. Stephen Coles the Director, she is a "Validated Super Centenarian," the oldest in New York State. Dr.Coles, reports that there are fifty-four Super Centenarians in the world, fifty females and four males. Researchers can't scientifically explain why female outlive males. They call it the female advantage. He said that researchers do know that longevity is inherited.

By the time Tee celebrated her 110th birthday, she was a celebrity. She appeared on national television several times, including Good Morning America. She was interviewed by reporters from The New York Times, The Daily News, and the Canarsie Courier. Tee was honored with several plaques and proclamations from the usual local politicians. These are just a few. Her District Congressman, The Honorable Edolphus Towns, placed in the Congressional Records these remarks honoring Tee "Mr.

Speaker, I rise today in recognition of Miss Susie Mushatt Jones for love of life and service to her children. Throughout her life she has been led by a basic principle of giving all that she has while living an upbeat life." One reporter asked Tee how she felt and what she liked about her life. Tee raised her voice and announced that she "liked cake, watermelon, bacon, and the fellows," meaning her preference for dealing with the males in her family rather than the females. Tee laughed along with everyone who was amazed at her sense of humor.

Andrew Cuomo, the Governor of New York, sent a representative to read his plaque in honor of Tee's milestone birthday, and it read, "I am delighted to send greetings and heartfelt congratulations as you commemorate the auspicious occasion of your birthday. Your energy and enthusiasm inspires all who have been so fortunate to know and love you, and I am honored to extend my best wishes for a memorable birthday celebration and many blessings ahead."

The last two years Tee was honored with visits at her apartment during the year and at her birthday parties by two groups of young children: The New York Housing Authority's Bay View Community and Public School 276 O.S.T. Summer Camp. The children serenade Tee with their sweet, young voices, read poems, and recite some of the historical events that occurred during 1899, the year Tee was born. Each student tells Tee their name and grade. They also try to engage Tee in a dialogue about her life and what it was like when she was growing up in Alabama. Tee encouraged each student to work hard and stay in school. Our aunt was in her glory as each student gave her a hug and told her they loved her. With a big smile on her face she responded, "I love all of you and I want you to come back to see me soon."

Those of us who knew Tee when she was strong, jovial, and happy, feel a sense of sadness seeing her body, mind, and spirit slowly succumb to the aging process. The last five years have been difficult for her, never mind how heroic and stoic she has been. This transitional period has been her abyss. Independent, strong-willed individuals, like Tee and her brother Callie seem to have the greatest difficulty accepting the aging process, as losing their independence, their health, and strong bodies, puts them at the mercy of others. Individuals in this category tend to rely on their own strength, will power, and whatever faith they have to get them through difficult times.

When Tee first lost her mobility, she moved around via the wheelchair, went almost any place she wanted, and stilled maintained some degree of independence. This little inconvenience she could accept and she did for a period of time. However, living in a world of total darkness began to affect Tee's personality. We began to observe episodes of regression; uncooperative behavior, anger, swearing, and begging for someone to take her "out of this damn place." We were constantly trying to reassure our aunt that she was in the right place and that we would never abandon her. Sometimes after she calmed down, she would meekly comment, "If you'll think I am in the right place, then I had better stay here." We then praise her for her cooperation and understanding. This is the time when a couple of us start looking for tissue, because it breaks all of our hearts to hear her use that helpless tone and give in.

Other times Tee threatened to check herself into a nursing home because she thought that might be the best place for her. We describe what she could expect during a typical day in a nursing home, none of which appealed to Tee. She had to abandon that threat. Those of us who are aware of Tee's needs realize that living with one of her nieces is not the best option. More importantly, changing her residence is not going to improve Tee's overall quality of life. Additionally, Tee's overall needs at this point are too extensive for one person to adequately handle. Old, blind, and wheelchair bound, she has lost the ability to do for herself. She needs what she already has, an environment appropriate for individuals with handicapping conditions and, in her case, around-the-clock care.

We knew that Tee wanted to live with a member of her family, believing it would help her to bear the pain of darkness in her everyday life. She questioned why God kept her here on earth in such agony. Our aunt vacillates between feeling lucky to have such a caring family to accusing us of abandoning her despite our attentive care and frequent visits. These paradoxical remarks are so common place, we have practically dismissed them. In, reality, Tee truly believes as big as the family is, with a range of skills and expertise, we ought to be able "fix" her situation and make life better for her.

Despite the sadness each of us feels when our aunt goes through these stages of anger and frustration, everyone has been supportive of the decision that Tee is in the right place. We also believe that these tirades are meant to manipulate and control. Regardless of where Tee goes, her behavior will not change; most likely it will worsen.

On a hot, steamy Saturday afternoon, July 6, 2013, the family piled into Tee's small apartment to celebrate her 114th birthday. The Senior Center scheduled its party a week later on Friday July, 12th.

The family's party was held in the afternoon, which gave us plenty of time to prepare Tee for what to expect. Nothing gives her more satisfaction than to hear that her family is coming to see her. She doesn't like to be rushed and doesn't respond well to surprises. She is determined to have some control over what happens in her life. By the time the family arrived Tee was in a receptive mood, greeting everyone joyfully. The family brought their usual homemade dishes: chicken, turkey, ham, ribs, macaroni and cheese, green salad, potato salad, peas and rice, peach pie, and cake. The delicious decorative cakes were made by Lois and our cousin Deseria Mushatt Ramos.

Following our meal, we sang "Happy Birthday to Tee and everyone ate cake. We talked among ourselves, and took pictures. Despite the constant chatter, Tee was napping. She never complained and actually seemed to enjoy her noisy family. The following day, she got up a little later than usual. Apparently, she was exhausted from her party.

A week later on 7/12/13, The Center gave Tee an elaborate party in honor of New York State's oldest resident whom they call "Miss Susie." There were colorful, welcoming banners and balloons everywhere. The guests included family, friends, fellow tenants, dignitaries, politicians, and a horde of cameramen and news media. Unfortunately, this party was scheduled for 11 a.m., a little early for Tee, who doesn't get up until around 9 a.m. Her care giver had to attend to several matters involving her client: waking her up, giving her a bath, getting her breakfast, and supervising her eating. Doris, Lois, and I arrived early that day to assist the care giver and began preparing Tee for what to expect.

For breakfast, Tee had two scrambled eggs, bacon, toast, and orange juice, and her medication. She consumed every morsel of food on her plate. With breakfast out of the way, the three of us began slowly and gently dressing her as we talked to her about the days' activities. She hadn't said one word to us since we arrived. We reminded her that it was her 114th birthday and The Senior Center was giving her a big party. One of us was in the midst of trying to get her dress over her head, another person was putting on her socks and shoes, while the third person talked to her. The first thing she said to us in her grouchy morning voice while we continued to dress her was, "I don't want a party." We pretended we didn't hear her. Then she repeated it, but a little louder, "I don't want a party." When she repeated it a second time, we stopped dressing her and looked at each other with that expression, "Oh Lord, Tee is going to give us trouble today." Doris and I sat down while Lois calmed our aunt down. She agreed to behave herself. Fully dressed, and looking beautiful and stately in her long black and white dress with matching hat, Tee held her head up high as she was wheeled in to greet a cheering crowd of approximately 100 guests and flashing camera lights.

Our Aunt Tee behaved remarkably well during the brief ceremony as she and her guests were entertained with songs and poems from the NYCHA Bay View Community Center, and Paul Curiale's Millennium Group. There were brief speeches by family members, friends, and the reading of several proclamations from politicians and others who praised Tee for many years of service to her family, her community, and the City. This was Tee's first time meeting her District Representative, Hakeen Jeffries (D-Brooklyn Heights). As he shook her hands, he said, "If I look as good at 60 as Miss Susie does now, I'll be doing fine." The program was a well-organized, inspirational, and festive affair, thanks to the hard work of Paul Curiale, Director of the Millennium Development, and Dee Pozzouli, Director of the Senior Center, and Tee's niece, Lois Mushatt Judge. Everyone sang "Happy Birthday" to Tee and presented her a beautiful birthday cake. Someone from the audience asked Tee if she had anything to say. Tee responded in a strong clear voice, "Thank all of you."

For the last four years, we observed a continuous decline in Tee's ability to remember names, voices, and recent incidents. Sometimes if she hears someone's name a few times and concentrates, she finally gets it. If there is any background noise in the room, it's useless to try to have a conversation with her. My sisters report that Tee has stopped asking about people whose names she doesn't hear on a regular basis. They try to keep family names in her memory by frequently asking her about them. Even at this stage of her life, with its poor quality, there are days when Tee has her wits about her and surprises everyone with pretty good recall. We are delighted to listen to whatever she can recall from long- or short-term memory, even her swearing, which we have been hearing for the last six years. If the incidents are comical, her sense of humor lights up the room and everyone has a good, hearty laugh, including Tee. Then some of us want to cry because for a brief moment we see a glimpse of our favorite, sweet aunt as we once knew her—bossy, talkative, funny, and happy.

Aunt Tee never regretted the personal sacrifices she made for her family and others over the years. She feels richly blessed and pleased with her contributions to society.

We are surprised that Tee hasn't spoken about her last schoolmate and good friend Bernice, whom she called Pete, who died a couple of years ago. Tee and Bernice talked on the phone two or three times a day. We think that Tee has forgotten her dear friend. I remember when we told her that Bernice had died; she never asked when she died or what she died from. Her response was, "Oh, Pete died?" We believe that Tee grieved for her friend, as she grieved for all the other loved ones she lost, privately. I have seen my aunt express a range of emotions; anger, disappointment, and happiness, but never grief.

Up until two years ago, Tee always asked about our children, and sometimes she had brief conversations on the phone with them about school, encouraging them to do their school work and make good grades. When the children became teenagers, other interests consumed their time and energy. Also, due to Tee's hearing loss, she would sometimes just hang up on the children and others, claiming she couldn't hear a word they were saying. If someone tells her the name of the parent, she remembers the name of the child. Also, for some reason we don't understand, she is able to hear and understand males' voices better than female voices.

While Tee was always affectionate, reaching out for a hug or a kiss on the cheek, she now actually craves the human touch; wants to hold our hands, feel our bodies, lie in our arms and cuddle up like a baby. Interestingly after Tee lost her sight, she began to use her hands to assist her in identifying members of her family by simply feeling the upper portion of their bodies. Whoever she touched, male or female, she told them they were fat. Unlike the eyes, the hands apparently can misjudge or distort actual body size. Such comments did not please the thin nor overweight relatives.

During family visits to Tee's house on Sundays, everyone has some special role to play in Tee's care. For example, her three nieces, Doris, Lois, and Selbra, bring different cooked dishes of her favorite foods for the week. Sometimes, our cousins Mac and Valerie will bring something special for Tee. While at Tee's house, each person performs some specific duty pampering Tee. Selbra may, for example, prepare Tee's dinner plate, while Doris sits and chat with her. Lois trims her nails and braids her hair. Tee's niece Myra, who drives from New Jersey almost every Sunday, takes care of her whiskers. While her "girls" are working on her body, Tee closes her eyes, puts her head back and thoroughly enjoys these two hours of pampering. When her pampering is completed, she opens her eyes and says, "Are you done already?" If she had a choice, Tee would surely duplicate this treatment every day of her life. Tee's need and desire for attention speaks volumes about her level of selfishness at this stage of her life. Perhaps this is because she spent a great portion of her life focused on the needs and comforts of others. In her declining years, the attention is all about what she wants and needs.

Aunt Tee has lived an exemplary life, for the most part, happy and healthy. We are not sure what to attribute this longevity to. It has been known for some time that longevity runs in families. We have documented that both of Tee's grandparents lived to be over

100. Our father, Callie, died at age ninety-four, and two thirds of Tee's siblings were over eighty at the time of their demise.

Tee has lived under the administration of twenty presidents, beginning with William McKinley, a Republican in 1889, to Barack Obama, a Democrat who was re-elected for a second term in 2012. The 114 years of Tee's life have been among the most fascinating, inspirational, and evolutionary in our history. There have been several wars, natural disasters, racial and civil unrest, inventions, discoveries, lunar explorations, development of vaccines, organ transplants, and other medical miracles. We have witnessed the investment of untold contributions and personal sacrifices of men and women, all in an effort to improve the quality of life and the longevity of the human person. Our Aunt Tee is among those individuals who made the ultimate sacrifice, by abandoning their goals to give others an opportunity to achieve their dreams. Tee says that she has no regrets and is proud of the beneficences of her sacrifices. She feels blessed to have lived long enough to see and enjoy some of the fruits of her labor.

Tee looks tired and lonely now sitting in her chair with her eyes closed. If she is not sitting near the window where she can feel the warmth of the sun, she will not know whether it's night or day. Then she must constantly ask, "Is the sun shining?" Or "What is it doing outside, is it raining?" When she first lost her vision, someone gave her a clock which announced the time of day every hour. After a few years Tee lost interest in just the time of day; she began to have a thirst for more details about what was going on in the world outside. She would ask, "Is my neighborhood a nice neighborhood? Are there people walking on the street?" At some point she asked one of my sisters how far she lived from her. Tee had forgotten that my sister lived only a few blocks from her. She feels alienated from the ordinary sights that sighted individuals take for granted. Blindness has robbed her of all visual stimulation, and with the passing of time she has forgotten what the environment looks like. I wonder if Tee would be able to recognize faces of family members at this point. Thank goodness she still has some hearing; otherwise, she would be living in a world without sound and sight. Therefore, continued conversation relevant to her environment is essential for Tee's emotional well-being. The family members who live near her are doing their best to meet that need.

We are astonished that as Tee approaches the end of her life, she has not broached the subject of her mortality with us. She only brings up the issue of death when she wants sympathy or is in a state of despair: "I wish I were dead." We know the details of what she wanted fifteen years ago, so we are assuming that she hasn't changed her mind. About eight years ago, Tee told us that she wanted to go home. We felt compelled to tell her that it was not her decision when she left this world, and the Almighty God was not ready for her at this time. Tee sat up in her chair. "I don't mean that home; I mean the home in Alabama." It occurred to us also that perhaps Tee wants to return home to Alabama to die in the place where she was born and where her family is buried.

We had a family reunion in Alabama in 2007; but Tee chose not to go. We believe she regrets missing that opportunity as she continues to ask us to take her to Alabama.

It's incomprehensible to us that a young girl growing up in Alabama during the early 1900s, who prayed and dreamed of leaving Alabama, who is now in the twilight of her life, burns with nostalgia to return to a place where everyone of her generation has passed on.

CAKES! CAKES! CAKES!

More Cakes!

CHAPTER 11

A SPECIMEN IN THE STUDY OF LONGEVITY

Are the secrets in the genes, lifestyles, environment, or something else?

I have documented when and where Tee's journey began and exampled some of the physical, emotional, psychological, and network systems that may have impacted her long life. She has been asked many times how she managed to live so long. Her responses are pretty consistent. What we know about her life and how she lived supports what research tells us. Apparently, in order for our lives to be meaningful and enjoyable, we must have a passion or commitment to or for something that brings comfort, happiness, and less suffering to others.

Life and living are purposeful; otherwise, we are like lost sheep wandering in the wilderness. People like Tee, with their big hearts and passion for the human condition are probably the happiest individuals because their work is never done. Someone or some issue always needs their attention. These individuals realize that their hard work may not make them rich, but it will certainly build pride, a feeling of success, and a great sense of dignity. Tee says she knows "hard work and struggles made me a better and stronger person, and even if I could I wouldn't change a thing."

What's unique about this woman, who grew up poor on a farm in the south, worked hard, earned little but gave so much for so long, yet managed to set the longevity bar so high? She is a role model and a trailblazer who just happen to be an exceptional human specimen. How does one explain the fact that Tee has lived longer than her ten siblings, her first cousins, classmates, and close friends? A close look at her life may give us clues. For those who think that living to be 114 years is awesome or impressive, below is Tee's recipe for longevity. Her lifestyle and perhaps her environment may be duplicated, but not her genes!

TEE'S RECIPE FOR LONGEVITY

- *Have faith and trust in a higher power*
- *Rely on your own faith and strength to get you through tough times*
- *Treat everyone with love and respect*
- *Have a passion and stay committed to it*
- *Stay devoted to family and friends*
- *Help others by sharing what you have*
- *Enjoy life*
- *Eat well and get plenty of rest*
- *Be prepared to work hard to achieve your goals*
- *Do something you can be proud of as you age*
- *Drink golden seal and sassafras tea*
- *Stay involved with children, they keep you young*

Gerontologists are still collecting and analyzing data in an effort to determine what factors are considered the standard or average for individuals who have arrived at the ripe age of 100-plus years. They want to know who these individuals are and how they managed to survive in a world exposed to diseases, stress, violence, harmful chemicals, personal obstacles, tragedies, and disappointments. Firstly, how will the increasing population of individuals living over 100 years impact the already broken

Social Security System? We will need to determine what physical, emotional, and psychological needs these aging individuals and their families can expect to encounter as we continue to live longer. Alzheimer's patients, for example, may requite care for decades. We will need to determine what role a series of variables play in the longevity paradigm.

We have begun compiling and accessing some of the known longevity variables in our family based on what we have learned from relatives and Tee' life. It is our impression that family genes, lifestyles, and environment provide the essential clues for understanding Tee's long life. We know that she began her life with a healthy, strong body and there was no history of her having sustained any serious illnesses. Despite having lived in her parents' home, where there were sick and diseased relatives, Tee had a healthy childhood. Tee and her siblings were not privy to pediatric care and early childhood immunizations. Because of the family's cramped living quarters, when one of the children became ill, usually the other children contracted the same illness. Tee was one of the hearty individuals who has enjoyed good health all of her life.

A study led by Paola Sebastiani and Dr. Thomas Perl of Boston University found a set of small DNA variations called genetic markers that they used to predict exceptional longevity with 77% accuracy. These researchers maintain that the vast majority of people's environment and lifestyle play a more important role in the aging process. Their theory is that only a handful of genes are linked to a long life.

We know from a growing body of knowledge that individuals who are actively involved socially, and able to avoid diseases and disability, live longer and have a better chance of aging successfully. Despite being isolated from her immediate family for many years, Tee stayed engaged with her friends, church, and social groups. She had to curtail some of her social activities as she and her contemporaries became too old to travel. At that point, Tee's family assumed a greater role in her life and care. Katherine Fiori, Ph.D., Assistant Professor at the Derner Institute suggests that individuals may give their physical and mental health a boost by cultivating the right type of social network. Tee seems to have orchestrated her life's journey by staying actively involved as long as she could.

Our Aunt Tee realizes that as the oldest surviving relative in our family, she commands the attention and affection of everyone. Despite her outbursts of anger and frustration, we know that she wants to placate us, because she loves us. Her physical being continues to inspire us. We love her and selfishly want her to stay on this earth as long as she can. Because she is a fighter, we know that she will.

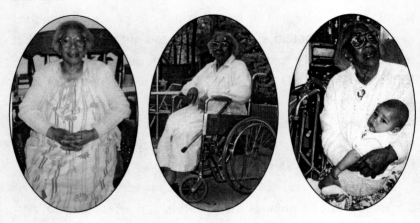

Tee — From 100 to 114

Uncle Roosevelt and Family - 1996

My sister Georgia, cousin Elliot, Bernice,
Ruth Lembeck at Tee's 97th birthday party

Lois, Georgia and Doris - January 2013

The family celebrates Tee's 100th birthday - 1999

Tee and her cousin,
Margaret - 1985

James (Sonny) Glover with
wife and grandchildren

Tee, Doris and great-grand niece. Lelia

*Darryl, Nia and Lydia at Tee's 110th birthday party
in the Bronx, NY*

*Tee's cousin Hildra Hayes and brother Callie Mushatt
in Alabama 2003*

Tyrone and Taheera Mushatt,
Callie and Jeanette's son and
daughter-in-law

Tygee Mushatt
Tyrone and Taheera's son

The 2001 Andrew's visit
Tee, Carol, Val, Joan, Mac, Audrey, Gail and Paul

Family and Friends at Susannah's 114th birthday July 12, 2013

*Young children from NYCHA Community Center
and Paul Curile's Millennium Group who performed
at Tee's party - 2013*

Paul Andrews (Tee's baby) 2013

Tee receiving a proclaimation from Brooklynn D.A. Hynes for her long life and service - Senior center 114th birthday celebration

Family and friends at Susannah's 114th birthday celebration in NYC. Jeanette, a friend, Val, Richard, Mac, Lois, Doris, Selbra, Bertha and Lavilla

The Watson Family
Zach, Lavilla, Susannah, Russ, Gloria, Audrey and Amber

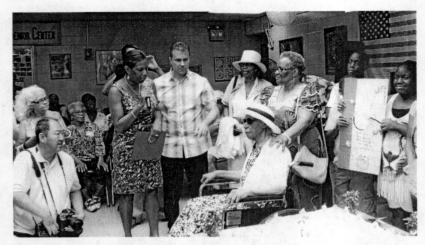

Tee accepts a citation from NY State Gov. Mario Cumo"s Representative for her 114th Birhtday Celebration. Her caregiver Cecily and niece are with her

Tee naps after her 114th Birthday Party

FAMILY
PHOTO
GALLERY

125

My Mother's Spareribs

...c 10 mi. .es 6.

4 lb Spareribs   1 tablespoon worchesterbw
1 onion   2 teaspoon chili powder
1 cup Ketchup   1 teaspoon salt
2 cup water   1 teaspoon black pepper
¼ cup vingar   ¼ teaspoon caylnn

Lay spareribs in a roasting pan mix all ingredients together and pour over ribs, cover pan and cook in moderate oven (325) degrees for 1½ hour. Remove cover from roasting pan last half hour, of cooking and baste at five Minute intervals,

Rice And Bread Stuffing

½ C. each Chopped onion and Celery

1 ½ C. Minute Rice

½ C. butter or margarine

2 ¾ C. Chicken broth

2 C Seasoned Stuffing Mix

2 tablespoons Chopped Parsley

Saute onion, Celery and rice in butter in large skillet until lightly browned. Stir in broth. Bring to boil. Reduce heat, Cover, and simmer 5 minutes. Stir in Stuffing Mix and Parsley. Let stand a few minutes until stuffing mixture is moistened

May be used as it is or used to stuff Chicken or Turkey.

California Pound Cake

2½ C. Self-rising flour

2 C. Sugar

1½ C Cooking oil

1½ tsp Cinnamon

1½ tsp Nutmeg

1 Cup Crushed pineapple (with juice)

1 C Chopped Nuts

4 egg yolks

4 egg whites, beaten until stiff

Combine Cooking oil, Sugar and egg yolks
Mix dry ingredients together and add to the oil
Mixture; Stir in Crushed pineapple and
juice; Fold in the egg whites that have been
beaten until stiff peaks form. Carefully stir in
Nuts and pour into a greased floured tube
pan.

Bake at 325 degrees 1 hour 15 minutes

About the Author

Lavilla Mushatt Watson, the family's historian and Tee's oldest niece, was able to attend college because of her aunt's generosity. Lavilla has always had a special bond with her aunt. The writing of this documentary of Tee's life is therefore a privilege for Lavilla and a tribute to her aunt for her love and giving spirit.

During the course of her professional career, Lavilla, a licensed school social worker, developed well-honed skills as a passionate advocate for children and parents. For her outstanding service in the field of Social Work, she received recognition from the Kiwanis Club, Woman of Excellence Award from the National Association of Negro Business and Professional Women, and was recognized by Nassau County, New York, for Outstanding Services to Families and Children of the Westbury School District where she worked. Lavilla was inducted in the Women's Basketball Hall of Fame in 2008.

She worked as an Adjunct Professor in Social Work at Adelphi and Columbia Universities in New York, where she trained graduates and undergraduates in the field of social work. For several years she served as a consultant to several organizations such as Health, Education and Welfare, Head Start, and The Parenthood Program.

In retirement Lavilla continues to participate actively in community and church activities. She has led workshops and sat on panels, committees, and advisory boards.

For four years, Lavilla researched, wrote, and published her family's history, The Journey From Gilchrist, A Family's History of Survival, Struggles, and Triumphs.

She received her Bachelor's Degree from Livingstone College, Salisbury, North Carolina; Master's Degree in Social Work from Columbia University, New York, Doctorate in Social Welfare from Adelphi University, Long Island, New York, and a Professional Diploma in Supervision and Administration from C.W. Post/Long Island, New York.

Lavilla is a widow who lives in Sarasota, Florida. She has two children and two grandchildren. Her favorite activities in retirement include traveling, spending time with family, gardening, reading, dining out with friends, and exercising.

CPSIA information can be obtained at www.ICGtesting.com
Printed in the USA
LVOW08s1242110214

373221LV00001B/8/P